A

STORY

OF

SEVEN

SUMMERS

# A
# STORY
# OF
# SEVEN
# SUMMERS

*Life in the Nuns' House*

# Hilary Burden

First published in 2012

Allen & Unwin
Sydney, Melbourne, Auckland, London

83 Alexander Street
Crows Nest NSW 2065
Australia
Phone:    (61 2) 8425 0100
Email:    info@allenandunwin.com
Web:      www.allenandunwin.com

Cataloguing-in-Publication details are available
from the National Library of Australia
www.trove.nla.gov.au

ISBN 978 1 74237 684 4

p. 253: 'The Round'. Copyright © 1985 by Stanley Kunitz, from *The Collected Poems*
by Stanley Kunitz. Used by permission of W.W. Norton & Company, Inc.

Internal design by Nada Backovic
Set in 12/16 pt Apollo MT by Post Pre-press Group, Australia
Printed and bound in Australia by the SOS Print + Media Group.

10  9  8  7  6  5

MIX
Paper from
responsible sources
FSC® C011217

The paper in this book is FSC® certified.
FSC® promotes environmentally responsible,
socially beneficial and economically viable
management of the world's forests.

If we can revise our attitudes towards the land under our
feet; if we can accept a role of steward, and depart
from the role of conqueror; if we can accept the view
that man and nature are inseparable parts of the unified
whole—then Tasmania can be a shining beacon in a
dull, uniform, and largely artificial world.

Olegas Truchanas, 1971

Direct your eye right inward, and you'll find
A thousand regions in your mind
Yet undiscovered. Travel them, and be
Expert in home-cosmography.

William Habington, 'To My Honored Friend Sir Ed. P. Knight',
in *Walden* by Henry David Thoreau

# PROLOGUE
## Tasmania, 2010

On the first day of spring I was asked to write about my life. I opened an email and there it was, staring back: an invitation, too shiny to read on my own. I called Barney and we continued to read it together arm in arm at the computer. As you can imagine, I felt flattered, and tearful, too. You might not have been asked to write a book but I'm sure you know that feeling. I think these are the sort of tears cried when a view or person takes you over and you can't explain it: tears of joy, of preciousness mixed up with dread for the hope of it and also the implicit loss, because moments truly lived are never eternal and you must inevitably let them go. I also knew that a life spent writing about other people's lives did not qualify me to write about my own. And yet, I would like to share the things I've learned from the privileged position of being allowed to ask nosey questions of interesting strangers as if I'd known them all my life. Ha, the impertinence of earning a living out of that!

1

What made me decide to change my life and risk everything? To go from working at the hub of London's glossy
magazine publishing world to a scruffy old house on an
island—alone? It's not easy to answer but, if I can share with
you some of the thoughts that were going through my mind at
the time, you might trust how the impetus for change may not
be an epiphany—more a slow-brewed search for something to
believe in.

So today is the most tender of days as I begin to see the
shoots of my story emerge with freshly minted self-knowledge.
Looking back over seven summers, I know that *who* I am is
*where* I am. It might not be the secret to life, but it is the secret
to *this* life. And if you were here, now, looking out on the day
through open doors and windows, you might smell jasmine
and rose on the cool morning breeze, mingling with the smell
of burned toast and ground coffee from the kitchen. A frisky
pair of wattlebirds darts through the copse, either playing or
fighting—who can tell? Jack and Kerouac graze with alpaca
indifference in the paddock. Marilyn and Monroe scratch about
in the garden; it's 9.30, they might have laid an egg each by now
but I wouldn't bet on it. And I can hear Barney across the road,
loading the mower onto his ute, getting ready to go gardening
up the road at the Pear Walk in Lalla.

These days, living in the country in Tasmania after a high-
rise life spent in cities, I have time and space for reflection that
is not so much accidental as crafted. I'll tell you how that came
to be and that will be the story of the Nuns' House.

# CHAPTER 1
## *London, 2004*

I used to live in a one-bedroom, third-floor Edwardian mansion flat overlooking a bridge on the River Thames. In winter, I could see as far up the river as Craven Cottage, Fulham Football Club's ground, and as far downriver as the spire of St Nicholas Parish Church, Chiswick. In summer, my view was of the leafy London plane trees whose roots lay somewhere under the concrete footpath. Sometimes you could hear the wood pigeons cooing, but mostly the sounds were of an endless drum of traffic from the road below. I don't remember ever seeing the stars in four years, but I loved to sit on the bench on Hammersmith Bridge at sunset or moonrise with a bottle of sparkling wine. It was a simple wooden bench made for any bottom that cared to sit there: a bench with no name.

I was born in Britain, brought up in Tasmania, and worked overseas for most of my life, while still calling Tasmania 'home'. I lived away—in Sydney, Tokyo and London—for over twenty years. 'Have you ever worked abroad?' was the question I wanted to answer with the YES of experience. So work became a home that was on the move and going places, a job with a salary and a wardrobe full of jackets. And my childhood left behind. Tasmania was where I learned how to shoot, go four-wheel-driving, scuba dive, line-fish for flathead, cook abalone and crayfish, steer a motorboat, sail a yacht, and hang-glide—mostly before I was old enough to vote. I used few of these skills in England. Maybe that's why I always thought something was missing. While dating the exciting kind of men you meet in big cities (bankers, lawyers, writers and politicos), I fantasised about a partner who could also throw a dog on the back of a ute.

Instead, the glossy magazine world in which I was absorbed took me to exciting places: a café opening in Venice, the launch of a new Chanel nail polish in Paris. I went from jet-boat racing at the Cannes Film Festival to canoeing down the Zambezi, and interviewed everyone from Kylie Minogue (recording her first single for Stock Aitken Waterman in a Bermondsey studio) to Kevin Kline on a plump sofa at the Mayfair Hotel and Elle Macpherson in a chic pied-à-terre in Paris. I was like a Polly-anna living a lily-pad existence.

For many years I thrived on these skin-deep moments, but eventually my spirit wore thin and I could not throw off the feeling that my life was false. I started searching for something I could not define, some version of the road less travelled, and found my sense of direction took me into churches. For a while, All Souls Church, Langham Place, next to the BBC's headquarters in Broadcasting House, was convenient to Great Portland Street where I worked. In my lunch hour I'd pop in to breathe a different air that comes with high ceilings and wide rooms. When Princess Diana died I recall an air of sadness so poignant I stood outside the nearest church to contemplate the space from a distance. Winchester Cathedral was also a favourite haunt, but that was more about architecture than religion. If ever there was a time for me to be 'saved' by religion, I suspect this was it. I guess I've never been the kind of person who puts their fate in someone else's hands.

Instead, every year I would escape to New York on my own for a long weekend, shopping for labels, sitting in hip hotel bars, walking the streets, exploring museums and galleries for inspiration and ideas from the city that never sleeps. I think it was Carrie's line in *Sex and the City*: 'In New York they say the only thing you're looking for is a job, a boyfriend or an apartment.' Maybe I was, but none found me. So I went to the other extreme and learned to ride a motorbike so I could ride solo across the Nullarbor from Perth to Melbourne. From the middle of everywhere to the middle of nowhere I looked for meaning and direction, finding neither. Road signs along the route explained, helpfully, YOU ARE HERE. Yes, I pondered, it's good to know where you are, but what does that mean?

Although for much of the journey the earth was blood-red and the sky true-blue, I took black-and-white photographs inspired by the solemnity of Ansel Adams' landscapes. At London's Hayward Gallery I'd recently seen his exhibition of stunning black-and-white images, taken over a professional lifetime, of Yosemite National Park, California. Of a moon over a winding road through textured wheat fields—a seemingly snapped moment, but, as the caption explained, one that Adams had waited days to capture. I know now that a life lived well is lived deeply beneath the gloss. But back then, I found myself sitting on a bench in the middle of the gallery unable to hold back tears, sobs of emptiness and morbid self-pity that drove me to misery, and finally therapy, because I could not stop the tears. 'Perhaps you were crying because you missed Australia and the images of the mountains and wide open spaces reminded you of home?' said the psychologist in one session. It sounded too simplistic and banal for me at the time. After all, I thrived on northern hemisphere thinking, craved a culture of intellect, revelled in sharp minds and articulate thinkers, and liked to swim in the zeitgeist. How could laid-back Australia compete? But the effect of things said is sometimes only realised much later.

'There are only seventy-two summers in one lifetime,' I remember a London ad man telling me when he left the safety zone of a big job to start up his own business with a friend. He said they'd named their agency 'Karmarama' and, while I wondered what exactly he'd be selling, the line he used stayed with me. If I only had thirty summers left—less if I was unlucky— then what was keeping me?

On the day of a solar eclipse, I went down to the river to watch the sun blacken, along with hundreds of others who lined the park by the Thames in the middle of the afternoon. I watched the moon pass in front of the sun and the randomly assembled crowd oohed and ahhed and whispered in unison, moved by something greater than themselves. After the sun had reappeared it took all the effort in the world for me to walk the short way home, as if I had to will and push my own blood through my body to keep living. What do I do now? *What do I do?*

The essence of my loneliness was that I wanted to be fully expressed and fully understood—and it wasn't happening. It wasn't happening in my work, or in my love life. And every step I took to meet the world seemed like a step that set me back. Every opportunity that sold itself was transient. Other people met men, got married, had children, bought homes together. My tendency was to meet people who offered the world and delivered the opposite. Marcelle was one friend who seemed to understand. As a former editor of British *Cosmopolitan* she had long been an advocate of the single girl's life, especially over a coffee éclair in our favourite haunt, Patisserie Valerie. 'Hil,' she asked, when we were dissecting why the man to whom I was engaged to be married had started an affair, 'do you think you'll ever be able to fall in love again?'

As a single woman in London, weekends were often spent shopping, walking or soaking up old movies on BBC2, either alone or with friends. I recall one Saturday afternoon watching three in a row, all by the 1950s director Douglas Sirk. My notes remind me now. They were *Magnificent Obsession, Imitation of Life* and *All that Heaven Allows.* And they all revolved around the single theme of finding your true and real path in life; once you find that, they promised, you will be lit from the inside. There were many times in my life when I thought I'd found that point, only to be disappointed and to return to the gnawing frustration that this is what life is and always would be: that some people lived lives that other people dreamed about and that I was to be one of the dreamers with a life unlived. As it happened,

*All that Heaven Allows* starred Rock Hudson and Jane Wyman and featured a book I'd never heard of, *Walden* by Henry David Thoreau. I ordered a copy and when it arrived devoured it.

> ## It is not worth the while to go round the world to count the cats in Zanzibar.

The fanciful line stood out and it was as if all the cats in all the cities I'd ever visited were haunting me now. I could see the skinny cats in Bali, the slinky Siamese in Marrakech, pampered cats in Parisian laps and cats on Roman holidays. I started thinking about moving out of the city, of fresh air, open spaces, and nature that was raw and wild.

After leaving Tasmania in a hurry in my early twenties to work first in Sydney, and then London, I never imagined that I would return to live there. People would joke that there were more sheep than people on the island and that the state's half a million inhabitants were all inbred. Over two decades, many a holiday was spent travelling the 17,000 kilometres back to Tasmania to visit family for Christmases or birthdays, or to introduce them to the important boyfriends, though never a husband. Wilf, my father, once remarked knowingly, 'Mark my words, you'll be a spinster aunt,' as if there was something rare or wrong in that. He could hardly know that in my world, the spinster aunt was the norm. Many of my friends were bright, independent women, flawed and funny doyennes of single life. In Tasmania, being a spinster aunt was nowhere near sassy, but I saw its other advantages. When you got off the plane, fresh air hit you in the face like a wet towel and you breathed differently there.

Gradually, over the years, an objective appreciation for things Tasmanian grew and I would return to my northern hemisphere life with pebbles and shells stolen from southern hemisphere beaches, and treasured photographs taken in front of wild oceans, in rainforests, on gravel roads. Following one particular trip, in the mid-nineties, I returned to London with a shopping bag of Tasmanian goodies I'd picked up on my travels: leatherwood honey in an old-fashioned tin, fresh rainwater in a plastic bottle, homemade relishes in jars, and small pouches of native pepperberry spices. I took the bag to the heart of foodie London: Conran's Bluebird Epicerie on the King's Road, Chelsea. The friendly food buyer was inspired by what I'd shown her from the other side of the world. 'Cloud Juice,' she said, referring to bottled rainwater from King Island. 'I could easily see that on our restaurant tables upstairs . . .' I don't know what I was hoping to achieve from the visit other than wanting to share what I thought was unique about the place I grew up in, a place that often got left off the map. My love of something as pure as rain captured from a tin roof and bottled was clear to me, but I had no desire to become a food exporter.

Instead, I continued working as a writer and editor specialising in launching new magazines. I liked the challenge of starting from scratch with a blank page. One of them, a new food title for the BBC's magazine division, was code-named 'Project Olive'. Breaking all the rules to do with codes, *Olive* fitted so well it actually became the name of the magazine. That was also how I got to taste truffles for the first time. Close your eyes and try to imagine the smell. It's like trying to describe the perfume your mother wore when you were three years old. More than a smell—it's a memory, like attraction itself. I tasted my first truffles in Umbria with a group of chefs and food journalists invited to the Urbani family's truffle estate in Scheggino. I took notes for a story as we went.

There are ten species of truffle gathered in Italy: the most prized are the white truffle from Alba, Piedmont, and the black truffle from Norcia and Spoleto. White truffle ripens from October to December, favoured by summer rains, and the black from November to mid-March. The white is more subtle and generally preferred raw while the black is usually cooked. It would take a poet to evoke their taste without using another taste to describe them . . .

One of the chefs was Curtis Stone. Even the men at the *Olive* magazine office had swooned when Curtis came in to discuss the trip, and now here we were squashed up next to one another on a minibus in Umbria. Curtis spoke Italian because he'd once lived in Calabria. Italians, he said, have the best attitude to food in the world because they live for their lunch. So, what is the best way to eat the world's best truffles, I quizzed. 'Shaved raw on to food,' was his answer. 'There's nothing better than the smell and flavour of thin slices of fresh white truffle just as they hit hot food. The white is amazing uncooked—so delicate—you should let it speak for itself.'

I liked the idea of letting things speak for themselves; that we had come to experience the pointy end of haute cuisine, in the place where it belonged, only to learn that *shaved raw* was better than any trick played by a chef. That evening we strolled the streets of Spoleto to find a camping stove, borrowed plates and cooking utensils from the hotel we were staying at, and packed a rucksack ready for what we decided would be a food shoot in the countryside. The next day, in search of truffles, Geoff, the photographer, Curtis and I travelled by bus into the Umbrian hills with Gianni Piermarini and his truffle-hunting dogs. We set up camp on the side of a hill and Curtis made a lunch of scrambled eggs where our truffles were found. This may have been my first introduction to a word I had yet to learn the meaning of: provenance. The truffle was a gift from this place.

For me, an appreciation of food was not about being a cook, a chef or a foodie. It was more about having an appreciation for where things come from and for knowing what makes something truly itself. I couldn't do this for myself without knowing where my home was. And when I asked myself honestly if it was London, it wasn't. Although I was born in Bristol, and Wilf and my mother, Audrey, were both Londoners, England was in my head, not my heart.

I had hit a rut in the city but didn't want to blame it. What I was looking for was the exact opposite of a packaged meal for one from the ready-made meals in Tesco Metro. I wanted to walk up the road to a real greengrocer, buy fresh fish from the fishmonger, have a yarn with the local publican, and wend my way home with fresh bread. I looked for this sense of home wherever I went, and seriously in Aldeburgh and Salcombe, but with no success. On one of these trips, I found in a second-hand bookshop a copy of William Hazlitt's *The Spirit of the Age*, contemporary portraits first published in 1825 of Jeremy Bentham, William Godwin, Samuel Taylor Coleridge, Sir Walter Scott, Lord Byron, William Wordsworth, Thomas Malthus, William Wilberforce . . . names that resonated with romance and vision. 'Mr Bentham is not the first writer who has assumed the principle of UTILITY as the foundation of just laws, and of all moral and political reasoning . . .' wrote Hazlitt, though adding, 'he has not allowed for the *wind*.' Wherever my independent life would take me next, I wanted to be both useful, and to allow for the wind.

I decided to take a holiday in Tasmania. I hadn't been back for a couple of years and organised to join a group on a four-day walk along the white sandy beaches of the Bay of Fires. By day, our group of strangers shared footprints in the sand and conversations were lost on the sea air. By night, around a campfire and under stars, we talked about youth and beauty. I became friends with Gillian, one of the walkers from Sydney, and she

*Remainders of a mussels lunch at the Bay of Fires.*

mentioned a documentary called *Wildness*, about two Tasmanians, the great wilderness photographers Olegas Truchanas and Peter Dombrovskis. Later, Audrey tracked down the video and posted it to me in London.

The philosophy of these two photographers was simple—if people could see the beauty of Australia's wild places they might be moved not only to protect them but to understand the true value of the world around them. It struck me that this message should be applied not just to the Tasmanian wilderness but to everywhere we live; that if we could see the beauty in anything we would then understand the value within.

I returned to London in midwinter and finally decided to put my small flat on the market and start searching online for a home in Tasmania. Who can say which one moment or revelation pushed me past the point of no return, to construct an argument to sell my flat and move across the world, letting go

13

of twenty years of friends and work hard won? But like Road Runner reaching the edge of the cliff, that point had come. In the beginning, one property seemed to beckon—an old weatherboard farmhouse on the east coast in the middle of a paddock, sheltered by a line of macrocarpa trees, overlooking a wild white-sand beach. Concerned friends thought it looked a little isolated, which made me feel the need to defend it, but instead I found myself saying, 'Well, yes, you're right, it is.'

I went ahead and organised a local surveyor's report on the property and when that came through, booked a ticket to Tasmania to view the house, just a few months after my last visit home.

# Curtis's scrambled eggs with white truffle

3 eggs
2 tbsp double cream
salt and pepper
a knob of butter
1 fresh white truffle
olive oil to drizzle
fresh crusty bread to serve


Crack the eggs into a bowl with the cream and whisk. Season with salt and pepper.

Heat a non-stick pan and add the butter. Once it starts to foam, pour in the egg mixture. Don't stir for 45 seconds, then once the egg starts to set, stir gently with a spoon.

As soon as the egg is nearly cooked, remove it from the heat. Slice the truffle over the egg and drizzle with olive oil.

Serve with the bread.

Serves 2.

# CHAPTER 2

## *Winter, Tasmania*

The farmhouse was a three-hour drive from my family in Launceston—a lot closer than a thirty-hour flight, but not too close. I decided to stay in the area overnight and found a secluded B&B right on the seafront just a short stroll away. Although the farmhouse was derelict and unloved, it felt like it held some sort of promise. I walked along the beach on that crisp winter morning and wrote the reasons why I thought I could live here in the sand. I loved how it seemed the sunrise did not want to end, and how the air felt permanently fresh.

The owner worked interstate and had a caretaker living in a caravan in the backyard. The agent explained that the property had been on the market for a while and that the owner was difficult to deal with. In fact, he wondered if the man really did want to sell. I made an offer that was knocked back. After a period of futile negotiating I realised it wasn't worth the agony of false hopes, and sadly withdrew my 'expression of interest'.

Friends reminded me that things not meant to be generally aren't, and I consoled myself with that. The house might have fallen through, but my resolve to move had not, and it seemed this setback had merely existed to test that I meant what I said.

The day before my flight back to London, still feeling stung by losing the farmhouse, I saw an ad in the real estate section of the local paper. I was spending my last twenty-four hours in Launceston at home with Audrey, where she'd lived on her own since separating from Wilf. I always remember my mother looking older than she actually was, with prematurely aged silver-white hair and porcelain skin that looked cracked by the Australian sun. She had legs made for miniskirts, though, and ever since I was young I'd wished I'd been born with her lips that she liked to colour in using Nutrimetics' 'Lobster Bisque'. We spent time potting pansies at her retirement home, baking impossible quiches, and sipping glasses of medium sweet sherry, which I only ever drank with her. For Audrey, the sign of a good recipe seemed to be how fail-safe it was, and when she made the quiche that seemed to make its own pastry as it cooked, I told her I thought it should be called Incredible Quiche. She couldn't remember where the recipe had come from, but I scribbled it down as she read out the ingredients. I liked the way she leaned on both elbows as she studied the page, and thought to myself that these were the things I would miss when she was gone.

'See, it couldn't be easier!' she said with a flourish as she finished reading the method that was all of one line.

More than anything, I loved the way Audrey's Wedgewood-blue eyes beamed when she saw you, and how she sometimes lifted her knee and slapped her thigh when you made her laugh, which, as I grew older, was often.

I was sitting in the sun on Audrey's front lounge, flicking through a newspaper supplement, when I spotted the tiny photo of a house in a paddock and a headline that read 'Character and Space'. I circled it with a pencil and said to Audrey, 'That's the kind of place I'm looking for. If you see something like that, let me know.'

'Oh, something like that?' she remarked. 'Where is it?'

'Karoola. Says here it's twenty-five minutes from Launceston . . .'

Audrey remained silent but seemed to be waiting while I took it in.

*Character and space*, I mused, I like those words. I looked at the photo of the weatherboard house and the way the large square windows seemed to look out cheerfully on the world.

**Karoola**

**Character And Space**

Large diverse character home built in 1898 with the flexibility of having three bedrooms plus or just lots of living space. Situate with a sunny northerly aspect and excellent rural outlook with views of Mount Arthur. Located on a little over 2 acres of pasture. The residence features French doors and ornate ceilings. Workshop plus 3 bay machinery shed. Ideal commuter property, around 25 minutes drive to Launceston CBD.

Enquiries Tom on 0419 369 162 or 6395 1546

Wait a minute, I thought to myself. I could arrange to visit today. There's still time. If anything, it would be a nice drive in the country. I rang the estate agent, Tom Dancer, and made an appointment to view the property in Karoola. He was also the Lilydale postmaster, he said, and would meet me after finishing his morning post run. We arranged a time and he issued me with instructions to 'set your speedometer at the Lilydale Road turn-off on Pipers River Road, and drive for 10.74 kilometres. The house number is 1074, on the right-hand side, corresponding with the distance. That's how the numbers work. Have you got that? I'll meet you there.'

I needed to go on my own, and Audrey didn't ask to come. I think she must have known that I wanted to have a view of the house that was mine and no one else's. I wasn't sure that Audrey would ever see what I saw, so I was pleased when she didn't insist. Perhaps she also understood how families could pull and repel at the same time and that if she pushed I might never come home.

The next morning, I watched as the gauge clicked over to 10.74 kilometres. There, on my right, just as Tom had said, was the house with the cheery veranda windows. It was a winter's day in late August, and the front paddock was cross-stitched with daffodils and jonquils. As I pulled up behind the agent's car, Tom Dancer was standing welcomingly at the front gate. He seemed more like a postman than an estate agent, warm but not overly friendly or sharp-suited. We shook hands and as he showed me up the front steps I noticed a rectangular brass plate on the front gate that read 'White Cottage', although the house itself was neither white, nor cottage-y. In fact, it was somewhat unexceptional, set on a sharp bend in the road, among rough paddocks surrounded by overgrown beds and borders.

Tom had already opened the front door, and as he showed me through the rooms it felt open and airy, despite old carpets that smelled of chequered family histories. I liked how you could stand in the centre of the house and see rural views to the front and to the back through doors and windows that opened wide. I could see a mountain through the large window in one bedroom, and imagined the moon appearing behind it. There was a walk-in pantry almost the size of the bathroom in my London flat. Inside another room was an old porcelain sink.

'It was a convent school at one stage, I believe,' said Tom. 'Nuns lived here. This would have been one of their bedrooms.'

Maybe it was the character, the space, or the French doors that opened up onto the wraparound, wide-screen valley view, but I knew from its outlook that this was the house I wanted. *You just know.* That's the cliché people use to reassure you when you're looking for a dream home, or at least the right place to live. It's a cliché because it's true. In fact, I had the feeling that this house had found me rather than the other way around. I wanted to call it my home and I could see myself here, waking up on the first morning, making tea and walking outside. I wanted to throw open all of the windows and doors, and, like a child, sleep in every room.

When I got back to Audrey's, Wilf was there on his usual Thursday visit. Although no longer living together, they had never divorced. Instead, he visited Audrey twice a week. They would often seem strained in each other's company. He was never particularly chatty and she had long ago given up trying to understand what was on his mind. How he must have felt like she was prying when she did. And how she must have learned to sink into herself in order not to make waves. She made him lunch, while he picked up the paper to finish off the clues that she couldn't get in the cryptic crossword. I thought, it's just how some couples are even when they're not estranged. I showed him the newspaper cutting of the house. He didn't appear taken with it, but when I told him it used to be a convent he lit up with laughter: 'You're going to live in a *nuns'* house!' Later, Simon and Jim, my two Launceston brothers, joined in the joke. Without realising it, they'd helped name my new home.

On the long flight back to London I resolved to contact Tom Dancer with a reasonable offer. With fingers crossed, I returned to work on the impending launch of *Grazia* magazine. Tom said he'd try to get back to me as soon as possible, although the owner was in hospital and hard to contact so it might take a couple of days. *Grazia* was still a secret project and a launch date had not been set. Over drinks in an Islington bar the Australian editor of the new weekly glossy asked if I had a photograph of the house. I took out the grubby and torn newspaper cutting I'd been carrying around in my wallet and gave it to her: 'Character and space,' Fiona read out loud. 'Oh yes,' she enthused knowingly, 'a good old Aussie house.' I was heartened by her response and felt she could see what I could behind the weatherboards and tin roof. Would the launch come first, I wondered, or the house purchase? I had to wait two weeks before I heard from Tom that my offer had been accepted and White Cottage was mine. I felt more relieved than ecstatic, as if everything had finally slipped, simply, into place.

I started imagining how the garden would be: all that space to play with. I bought the Royal Horticultural Society's *Good Plant Guide* of over 3000 recommended plants and placed stickies on the pages: on lupins, allium and bamboo, lily-of-the-valley, forget-me-nots and amelanchier, only to stop when I realised I should wait until I knew what grew in Karoola. These were *English* plants. What about natives? With this thought, I felt a shift in my thinking. Not to try to plant my future before it had even arrived, but to be patient and allow the future to unfurl itself. As I sat in my flat above Hammersmith Bridge, disentangling my roots from the concrete footpath, a different consciousness was forming. I was letting go of everything that had gone before, and putting expectation and planning to one side. I knew that in order to live in another place on the other side of the world I needed to resist what had gone before, or at least not attract it. That's how I learned not to spend every waking minute imagining how I would live at the house, or what I would do to it. I was determined to start with a blank sheet and wait until I got there. I didn't know what I would do in Tasmania, or how I was going to earn a living. But I knew I had roughly six months to decide—when my savings would run out.

In October, I waved goodbye to my worldly goods and chattels and, when the removalists managed to break the glass in a painting while packing it up, hoped that I would see everything in one piece in six weeks' time. By this time the London winter was closing in and I was feeling light-headed and ready. Yes, I was working on the inside of one of the most exciting magazine launches in the UK, but all my attention was in a paddock on the other side of the world at a place I now called the Nuns' House.

My flight was booked for early December and I said my final farewells to my closest friends over drinks at a trendy Notting Hill bar. Whatever doubts anyone held for me, I tried to reassure them by saying I'd be coming back often enough for work. I said it, although I wasn't sure it would turn out to be true. All I knew was that I was taking a simple step on a different path at a new address. And that it felt right. If my family had any doubts about my move they left them unsaid. The only thing they questioned was why it had taken me so long. In itself, the decision was never the hardest part of my journey. That was over the next horizon, in the unravelling of what on earth I was going to do next.

The week before leaving London I walked past the windows of Bond Street's boutiques. A pair of shoes caught my eye: scarlet, patent leather, three-inch stilettos. They were so perfectly sculpted and symbolic of every extreme that I wanted to photograph them. Three silver buckles were attached to three thin straps, and the bottom of the pointed heel was smaller than the diameter of a pen. More than *femme fatale*, these were killer shoes. Would they find a use in rural Tasmania? I tried them on and said to the sales assistant, 'They look like high-class prostitutes' shoes!' 'Yes,' she said, 'they really suit you,' and we laughed because they did. Like all the best shoes, they looked unfeasible off, but felt like slippers on. They were so much a part of the life I was leaving behind that it didn't seem ludicrous to want them, especially on sale for a third of their normal price. A good omen, I thought, as the West End shop assistant wrapped the red shoes in tissue paper and packed them into a box, ready for their migration south.

On the day I left London, 6 December 2004, George W. Bush had been re-elected President of the United States, aid workers in

*London shoes.*

Iraq were being taken hostage and their gruesome executions videoed for all to see, while the inescapable narratives of Jade, Jordan, Brad and Angelina were making headlines—as if it mattered. The news seemed either horrific or ridiculous.

My friend Lizzie drove me, once more, to the airport. I'd been her tenant, then friend, over many years. She was in her fifties, and in the decade or so that I'd known her our friendship had been as solid as a rock; she was the sister I never had. I'd signed a letter for her to keep as my preferred next of kin explaining that if the plane went down I wanted her to have everything: my home not yet a home, and everything that I owned in boxes currently somewhere at sea. We'd planned on a G&T at Heathrow, but once the unexpected issue of excess baggage had been sorted out, there was no time left for that. I don't know how it was for Lizzie but my leaving felt no different to the last time: a turn, a wave, final eye contact . . . and so on to customs. The only difference was that all of my worldly possessions were ahead of me. When I boarded the plane the Singaporean air steward asked where I was heading.

'Australia,' I said.

'On your own?'

'Yes, on my own.'

'Ah, so free and easy.'

When the plane finally landed in Launceston, I had the feeling of rising and sinking into a horse's saddle, *the right way*—relaxed, tension gone, not trying but knowing, a feeling of calm, of not missing, of balance. Plain and simple. As I peered out of the window the same way I had always done on returning to the island—scanning the heads waiting on the

airport balcony for Audrey's white hair and Wilf's height, pac-
ing—the words came over the intercom: 'Ladies and gentlemen,
we have now landed at . . .'

'Home,' I thought to myself. 'I've come home.'

# Audrey's impossible quiche

1 chopped onion
2 rashers bacon, chopped
1 cup of whatever you like (I like to add handfuls of whatever
herbs are in the garden and grated zucchini)
4 eggs, beaten
¼ cup butter (melted)
1 ½ cups milk
½ cup self-raising flour
1 cup grated cheese
salt and pepper
cayenne pepper

Place sautéed onion and bacon and the whatever you
like in a large bowl. Add eggs, butter, milk, flour
and cheese and mix well. Season. Pour the mixture
into a greased ovenware dish. Cook in a moderate
oven (180°C) for approximately 30 minutes.
Sprinkle with cayenne pepper on serving.

# CHAPTER 3

## First summer, Tasmania

It was early in the morning when I finally arrived at my new home, twenty minutes' drive from Launceston. I'd picked up the door key from the agent in town the day before, and stayed the night at Audrey's.

'Are you sure you don't want to head out now?' she'd pressed.

'No, it's late. I want to start out on a brand-new day. I'll be leaving early so I won't wake you.'

I packed up my Jeep Wrangler, remembering the bag of cleaning cloths and sprays that Audrey had left out for me. She had never been a champagne kind of mother. It was just on daybreak and I started the engine gingerly so as not to wake her. I'd bought the Jeep from a central Sydney car dealer, the first vehicle I had ever owned new, and travelled down with it on the overnight ferry from Sydney to Devonport. I chose a Jeep because when I test-drove it through Double Bay it roared like a four-wheel-drive rather than purring like a sedan in four-wheel-drive clothing. And I loved its engine power, the chunky lines, and how it reminded me of real army jeeps in *M\*A\*S\*H*.

As I turned off the main highway into Pipers River Road, I felt tears, joined-up tears of joy and arrival and meaning and heart, as if I were about to meet a new lover after spending weeks apart.

The drive along Pipers River Road was fairly flat and non-descript and the bush mostly scrubby, until I got to a bend in the road where the view opened up and out over the valley and swept right through 270 degrees, taking in the magnificent slopes of Mount Arthur. A sharp downhill right-hand bend overlooked a hillside of emerald-green pastures dotted with black cows; I thought it looked like Switzerland or Ireland before I told myself to stop comparing. YOU ARE HERE, I thought, it means something now. Like Thelma and Louise I felt like driving right off into that green hillside bosom view—but that was just joy talking.

Just get there, I found myself muttering. There was another bend, then another, and finally the right-hand turn into the driveway.

The outside air was still and fresh. I wanted to run up the steps but told myself to slow down, there was no rush, that I should take it all in. As I held the key to the front door in my hand the silence seemed to echo around the small porch. A black-and-white sign was stuck to the front door, like a surgery's: *Please ring*. But there was no bell to ring and no knocker. As I put the key into the lock I noticed that it was just a normal silver key. Why not big and old? I stepped inside to open up the doors and windows I'd held in my mind for all those months in London. *Breathe in now. And out. Yes, I'm home.*

I stood in the large front lounge room. Morning rays were streaming through the enclosed sunroom and hitting the French doors that opened out onto the view of an elbow-like bend and a mile-long road. Through watery eyes I tried to take in the view from the front veranda, broader than my peripheral vision, of a soft green valley like a runway for giant hobbits. Farm fence lines and long gravel driveways intersected with zigzag Pipers River Road, stands of gums were proudly vertical, there was a sweeping eyebrow of low-slung hills, and the omnipresent dolomite rock face of arching Mount Arthur. I knew I was home because I felt it. In part this was because of the view. I could see what was in front of me and I knew where I was.

A friend once introduced me to the English psychoanalyst Darian Leader. I recall his opening small talk. He didn't ask what I did or where I lived, but, 'How would you describe the view where you live?' 'Well, open and light,' I replied at the time, intrigued by his unusual approach to conversation, but I guess he'd had a few of them and knew how to sidestep the superfluous. Then, I was living in my small flat by Hammersmith Bridge overlooking the river. Now, here in Karoola, I imagined that, for many of my country neighbours, their view was what they did—farmers who woke with daylight and who lived the day.

Although the house was close to the road, I wanted to live privately, in a sanctuary. At the same time I didn't want to be shut off like a hermit. I didn't yet know how I would survive, but I knew I wanted to shed the stuff I associated with cities: suits, masks, labels, credit cards, microwaves, going out, dressing up, being very important or busy or loud. I didn't want to *have* to be anywhere, make plans, or be called upon really very much. So, *please ring*? That sign at the front door had to go. I started chipping away at it, feeling like a vandal.

'Audrey was right after all,' I thought to myself with a smile. 'It starts with cleaning.'

I spent the first day wandering from room to room, taking in the emptiness, contemplating what needed to be done, inside and out, accompanied all the while through open windows by a chirpy family of pretty electric-blue wrens who bounced from fence post to shrub.

The colour spilled out of that first day slowly and it was nearly ten o'clock before the stars came out to play. I took a blanket and lay in the paddock away from the house to view the night sky. Like my smile, those first-night stars were spread from ear to ear. Happy frogs and crickets sounded in the foreground, and I could hear the nearby river flushed and running with early summer rains. Although I was on my own, it felt like I had company. There were at least five homes within sight of the Nuns' House, a number that seemed to double at night when the lights of farms and houses popped out from distant hills. I didn't feel the need to make friends, but I did sense that we shared something, living in this landscape, as if we were all in it together, looking after it. It wasn't like living in a city where you could close a door on the outside world and disappear, or pass a neighbour on a staircase and not say hello, or look out of your window at blocks of flats and not know one soul living in them. It wasn't anonymous like that. Here, the country made you part of it. I had a sense that I belonged without being born here.

Karoola had a postcode but no shop, and the nearest village was seven kilometres away, at Lilydale. I didn't want to make too many comparisons, but in London the nearest corner store was a minute's walk away under Hammersmith Bridge, and there was a choice of three supermarkets within a five-minute stroll. To fetch supplies now I had to get in the Jeep and drive down the long stretch I could see from the front veranda. Turn right at the Karoola Hall, cross the bridge and decommissioned railway, then skirt around the edge of Brown Mountain via Lalla, the slope of Mount Arthur directly ahead, past Providence Vineyard, across the railway again, turn left at the police station and pin-neat war memorial into Lilydale Road, then past the district school, the 1950s memorial hall and the bull paddock. The drive to Bardenhagen's, the local supermarket in the centre of town, with the year 1888 marked above the front corner doors, took roughly ten minutes.

It seemed like you could get most things here. The people who served behind the counter were busy, kind women and I could tell the genuine locals because the shop assistants greeted them by name. 'If you can't see what you want,' said the friendly lady at the checkout, 'let us know, we'll try and get it in.' How

33

did she know the moment I walked through the door that I was new to the district?

'Got your shopper?' she asked. 'No? Another plastic bag then. I use them for my rubbish so it's not wasted.'

At the garage-cum-hardware store up the road, a man with a face the colour of outdoors introduced himself with an Aussie flourish. 'I'm Rob. They call me the unofficial mayor of Lilydale!' Along with 'Full Driveway Service' Rob seemed to sell mostly what was not at Bardenhagen's, including fence posts, mushroom compost, paint and kitchen plugs.

'I'm good for top-ups,' he said helpfully, placing the petrol cap back where it belonged.

I needn't even have left the driver's seat, but as I followed him inside to pay for the fuel, the petrol station and hardware store turned into a museum of memorabilia. Old-fashioned bowsers, oil cans and wheels lined the walls, and vintage posters too. Patsy Cline played on the music system and out of the corner of my eye I noticed a digital-image processing booth. If you asked for a haircut he'd probably give you one.

'Busy day today?' I asked as I paid him.

'I'm not wearing these shorts for nothing,' he quipped.

Now that's what I call service with a smile. As I drove back through the town I noticed a pub with bakery café, a hair salon, a takeaway, Tom Dancer's post office-cum-estate agency and gift shop, an antiques store, and a patchwork and quilting shop. I stopped at the chemist where I waited while a pensioner paid off fifty dollars on her account: 'That leaves thirty,' said the pharmacist, lowering her voice. 'Pay the remainder when you can manage it, that's okay.'

For the first week or so, the only furniture I possessed was a single foam mattress I'd borrowed from Audrey. I revelled in the simplicity of having nothing, waking with the sun, working through the day, and sleeping when it was dark. I ripped off the floral padded fabric that covered the pelmets and caught the dust, and pulled down all the old curtains to take to the op shop. There was a musty old dog smell which I worked out came from the carpets, so I started ripping all of them up, too. The rubber underlay was stuck to chipboard, there was ratty lino underneath that, and under all the layers I could see sturdy wooden floorboards. Each day, after pulling and rolling up lengths of carpet, I fell straight to sleep, physically exhausted. Once my furniture arrived in boxes with London stamped on the side, the days just became fuller. I went through the phone book to find a floor sander who could make it before Christmas and booked him.

I liked to leave the front door open to the day, so there was no knock, just a voice. He said his name was Glen and that he'd come to sand the floors. He was unusual looking, a pre-Raphaelite, twenty-something boy-man, tall with long corkscrew curls and fair skin. I played music as he worked—Nina Simone, Louis Armstrong—songs he'd never heard before, so he took his MP3 player out of his ears to listen. He said he liked 'He's Got the Whole World in His Hands' and asked me to play it again, so I did. I'm not sure if it was the words that caught him or the voice of Nina Simone: sombre, soulful, measured.

Sanding was hard work. The floors were scraped, peeled, sanded, scythed back, stripped of decades of domesticity and, before that, school life, revealing what's commonly known as Tasmanian 'oak' but is actually beautiful, honey-toned hardy

35

eucalyptus. With bare feet on bare old boards I felt the weight of the house lifted and life grounded. The next day, Glen brought some of his CDs for me to play, but before starting work again he said he had something to tell me.

'Let's sit outside,' I said, not sure what was to come.

'It wouldn't be right if I left here today without telling you that I really like you and that I've never met anyone like you in my life,' he said.

I was astonished at his directness, and all I could think to do was thank him for his honesty and the compliment. Every day since being here I'd felt younger. Was this man half my age a reward? Perhaps the house had cast a cheeky spell? I imagined the pent-up temptations of a nun's life and how they might be rushing in now that the house was being cared for and stripped back, nipped and tucked into new life. I told Glen that my focus, while soft and fuzzy, was on my new home, and it didn't include a man. Well, not now. Not yet. He said he understood and went back to work.

As I started to colour in the details of my new home, my travels and conversations were shaped by wanting to uncover its secrets. Through visits to local libraries and archives I found out that in the nineteenth century, Karoola had been one of many stations on the North East Railway line, and Pipers River Road

*Karoola orcharding country, published 1 July 1920 in the* Weekly
Courier, *photograph by F.V. Robinson. (Launceston Local Studies
Collection, Tasmanian Archive and Heritage Office)*

was known as 'the track from Launceston'. The area was first
opened up for timber harvesting and in the 1880s there were
three licensed hotels in the district. On 16 December 1898, *The
Monitor*, a Catholic newspaper, reported on the opening of the
new Sacred Heart Church on the hilltop behind me. The view,
it described, consisted of 'fields of waving corn and well tilled
paddocks' that gave it 'a picturesqueness difficult to surpass
anywhere in Tasmania'.

Later that day, after Glen had left, I strolled to the top of
the hill to take in the same long view out over the Pipers River
valley. As I opened the small gate to the churchyard cemetery, I spotted a fallen vase or two, and stopped to return a

spray of plastic roses strewn across a grave. Many of the names were Irish, some families lying together, and I imagined by the dates on the headstones that the McGrees and Connollys, the McCarthys and Flynns buried here were early pioneers. One sad memorial stone lay outside the graveyard boundary, near a tree by the church, remembered, yes, but not quite as one of them.

I learned the house was built around 1900 and was bought by the Karoola Sacred Heart Church in 1953. It was blessed and opened as a convent for the Presentation Sisters by the Archbishop of Tasmania, the most Rev. E.V. Tweedy. At one stage, the Sisters taught up to seventy pupils here, with the front veranda enclosed and turned into a classroom.

There were no photographs of the house itself. It was enough to know that it had been lived in, once, by single women of an independent spirit and moral purpose, and children had come here to learn. I hoped that the Sisters were kind, imagining how they might have cared for the gardens, that they cooked and sewed while helping to nurture a community's spiritual needs. In the archives I found a leaflet published in 1993 to commemorate a community reunion.

The photocopied pages told how the Sisters would tour the district in a pony and rig, helping people through everyday hardships, meeting the train to pick up children from remote areas travelling by train to school, and picking up supplies and visitors. Sisters who were ill often came to Karoola to recover in the fresh country air: a sanctuary even then. The leaflet told how the Sacred Heart Convent School was closed in 1958 and moved to a new venue at St Anne's in Lilydale to expand their teaching. The last nuns stayed on until 1968, when their superiors decided it was better for them to live in a larger community.

Conversations shone more light onto shadows. I met a neighbour who shared the kind of memories neighbours do in the country. Margaret was proud to be born in this valley but uncertain why anyone would want to know about the Karoola General Store, as it had been closed, she told me, for fifteen years. You would never have thought that it had once been the hub of the district, she said, how it sold everything from gentlemen's suits to a box of nails. With a sparkle in her eye, she recalled the smell of coal from the 'rail motor', all cream and green, on its way from Launceston through Pipers River to Turners Marsh, Karoola, Lalla, Lilydale and on to Herrick, busy stations that no longer existed now the railway line was closed. She also told me that my house was built by the Nicholls family, and that they were retirees from the British Raj in India who came here to establish orchards. My heart warmed as she opened up her childhood memories of walking past White Cottage on her way to school and peering into its 'secret gardens' surrounded by rhododendrons, camellias and 'those other lovely flowering trees in spring'.

'Magnolias?' I queried.

'Yes, that's right, magnolias.' She smiled. 'Oh, and tall macrocarpa trees. It really was quite beautiful.'

The gardens had not survived the decades. The macrocarpas had been cut down—only their stumps were left behind, covered with giant knots of ivy and ferocious blackberry canes so well established they had strangled and brought down small trees. The rough sloping garden seemed a mystery to me, made more out of focus by knee-high grass. The house had been unoccupied for some time and there were three months of spring growth to attend to.

A week after I'd moved in, my father Wilf arrived, as promised, followed by two of my three brothers, Jim and Simon, and Simon's sixteen-year-old son, Joseph, otherwise known as Joe. Three cars with trailers carting mowers, whipper-snippers and saws were lined up in the driveway. I could see Wilf sizing up the two straggly gutter-high fuchsia bushes at either side of the front porch.

'I think I'll get rid of them,' I said without thinking.

'They're warhorses,' he said. 'I wouldn't lose those—they're the few shrubs that have survived! All they need is a good hack.'

Wilf had always had an overreaching abundance of energy. It's probably what brought us to Tasmania all the way from sixties Bristol to the small north-east village of Derby where he worked as a country doctor while Audrey looked after four children, all of us aged under ten. To me his drive had always been at the heart of the family, while Audrey's quiet resistance must have been a force to be reckoned with. Now, while the three boys got to work slashing and mowing the grass, I noticed that Wilf was less active than I remembered. He seemed to hobble around on the edge of things, bending only to pull out a weed or identify another branch for Simon to prune. 'It's my dickie knee,' he said, by way of explanation, refusing to expand on this. I wanted old Wilf back, the man who sometimes greeted you with arms outstretched like Fred Astaire. Still, while slow-pacing his way around the garden, hands clasped behind his back, Wilf claimed a bit of the garden as his own: a wild bank held up by a dishevelled dry-stone wall, a screen of scrub so untamed it was impenetrable. 'Okay, that's mine, leave that bit for Wilfie,' he said, perhaps seeing the magic garden it might once have been. 'Oh boy . . .' He seemed to lose himself in the task ahead. I think he might have known that it would take more energy than he had or time to give.

We sat on the back lawn in the shade of a tree and stopped for a cold beer and a chunk of fresh quiche made by Simon's wife Karen. My sister-in-law had grown up with a mother who was always able to miraculously produce a table of sandwiches, scones, Welsh rarebit or rock cakes whenever visitors arrived. It didn't matter to Coralie what time of day it was, there would always be something to put out as a welcome. The only recipe I could remember learning how to make as a child at Audrey's side was fresh mint sauce. Karen's resulting confidence in cook-ing had always been a contrast to my own and she had once worked as a qualified chef. Her spiral-bound recipe collection, with a photograph of a perfectly sliced avocado on the cover, had been one of my staples ever since she'd given it to me one Christmas, and I loved to thumb through it to find the crumpled and stained pages that marked the recipes I used the most— comfort food like *Chilli con carne* and blueberry muffins.

By the end of the afternoon, the lawns were neat and trimmed, fence lines cleared and pebbled paths revealed. There were differences of opinion about what could go or stay. 'You have to be ruthless to achieve beauty,' Simon said. I told him I preferred to err on the side of wildness—at least until I knew what I was looking at. The day had been a whirlwind of male energy and, although I appreciated their physical efforts, I was grateful when the utes and trailers drove out of the Nuns' House driveway, leaving me to wonder about the garden's rehabilitation and the help I would need to get rid of the blackberries.

I booked a garden maintenance company and a minivan of men spent two days cutting back the blackberries, piling up the canes, rotting trees, layers of bark and detritus. Every job seemed to create another and I wondered how I was going to get rid of the mess. As the bonfires brooding on Pipers River Road showed me, the most efficient way of clearing dead scrub and unwanted garden rubbish was to burn it. So I made a test spot in the backyard, roughly the size of a car tyre laid flat and the exact size of my courage. I scraped the area clear of grass, filled a bucket of water as a precaution, lit the newspaper, covered it with a few dry twigs, and stood back. It's the sound that terrifies as fire takes hold. At this rate, days of burning-off were ahead of me, but all I could cope with was this small crackling campfire before fear doused it with a bucket of water.

Eventually, a helpful neighbour introduced herself and showed me how to 'groom' the fire before lighting it; to mow the grassy surrounds before starting, to keep watch over it, rake in hand, and attend to the embers as the flames waned so that everything was burned.

Except for a few showers, every December day so far had been sunshine-filled. I started putting tankwater on the garden but it was rain that made the real difference. Plants seemed to perk up differently; they liked water, but they loved rain. In my London flat, I'd never thought about water—had no idea where it came from, what was added to it, or how it got up to the third floor of Digby Mansions and into the pipes. I just turned on a tap and paid the quarterly Thames Water bills. In contrast, the Nuns' House relied on rainwater. It was pure, unadulterated (apart from what lurked in the gutters), free and unpredictable. I knew it came straight from the silvery roof that was steep and corrugated, and, when it rained, the sound on the tin filled my heart like a well. People I met who knew about rainwater liked to ask about the size of the tank and how full it was. In my mind, I hadn't yet joined up the rain and the reservoir with my own responsibility, so the sooner I found out, the better.

An old hut sat in the lower-front paddock made out of four rickety fibro boards that you could see straight through. Inside sat a small pump that was attached to a bore. When I bought the house, Tom Dancer said he thought the bore hadn't worked for a long time, so I called a pump expert to seek advice. When Hugh, a kindly man with big weathered hands and white hair, came to view the pump and quote for the job, he spent time in the garden as if he were trying to see through it. He shook his head knowingly, and tutted about the work ahead of me that I was only just starting to see for myself.

'It must have been a lovely garden once,' he said. 'Look, these are Dutch elms. They'll self-seed if you leave them. Just keep editing them back and they'll turn into a lovely copse.' A copse was something I'd kicked leaves under on Hampstead Heath—fancy having one of my own.

It turned out that all the pump needed was a new part, which meant that when it was fixed I would be able to water the garden as much as I liked with water pumped up from 35 metres below ground.

43

Each day I worked with my hands answering the needs of this house, leaving only to get necessary supplies from Bardenhagen's in Lilydale. To leave home without a reason felt, somehow, like a betrayal, a wanton waste of time. To go beyond my own boundary would be to lose momentum and turn my back on the things I'd started. It would be as if those small wins over weeds and water had counted for not very much.

One day, arriving home from Lilydale with nails, bread and sandpaper, I turned into the driveway to find a stray dog at the front gate—a smart Jack Russell terrier who seemed to think I owned him. I asked a neighbour if she knew whose dog it was. She thought he might belong to someone down the road at Lalla or maybe up near Austins Road in Turners Marsh. I opened the Jeep tailgate and he jumped straight in. His total acceptance of me was disarming. The dog didn't belong at the house in Lalla, where we were greeted at the front gate by a Jack Russell terrier whose name was Digger. We had no luck at Austins Road either. But on the way home I saw a man in a front garden and pulled up. 'I've found a lost dog.'

'Is that Digger?'

'No, I've already checked.'

'I could swear he was Digger. Where did you find him?'

'He was in my driveway when I came home.'

'Where do you live?'

'Near the Sacred Heart Church, on the big bend.'

'I know the one. Oh, you're there, are you? Good luck then.'

And off I drove with the dog, back to Bardenhagen's, to buy dog food. When I came out of the store, I found him nuzzled into a towel on the front passenger seat, looking right at home.

The next day, as we sat in the garden, me reading a newspaper with the sun on my shins, and the dog at my feet with an old scrap of dead possum carcass he'd scruffled from somewhere, a car pulled up and a tearful woman got out of the passenger side.

'Have you seen a little dog? A Jack Russell?'

'Yes, I have actually. He's right here!'

And the young woman with boyfriend in tow burst into tears. She'd been looking for him everywhere . . . he'd fallen off the back of the Toyota . . . it's new . . . he wasn't used to it . . . he's just like a human being . . . Oh, and the man on the hill up the road had told her she might find him here . . .

Over lunch at Simon and Karen's the following Saturday, Karen asked a question I'd never asked myself.

'Hil, do you ever think about what your life might have been like if you'd never left Tasmania? Do you think you might have wasted twenty years away?'

I told her truthfully that such thoughts had never crossed my mind. That if they did I'd be rocking with the regret of it all. None of what went before was wasted or being replaced. Not at all. Every border crossed, all the men kissed, and frogs too, the comings and goings, the broken hearts and soaring spirits, all the dreams and facials, and stamps in passports, every single gulp of breath I took had led me here, up this road, to this mountain view, and nothing that happened in between the years of brazen youth and burnished middle age was pointless because where would I be now if I'd never left?

After lunch I took a seat on the lounge next to Ray, Karen's dad, a wise old country railwayman. He told me he used to be the stationmaster at Herrick in the days when red lanterns were used at station platforms to signal to oncoming trains. I thought he might appreciate the story of the Jack Russell who got lost and turned up in my driveway. Ray sat forward in his armchair. 'Yes,' he said nodding. 'Yes. That's how it works.'

There was something comforting about that phrase—*that's how it works*. I took it to mean *like night follows day*. That night I lay in bed and thanked the day. I'd found a space where everyone might be helped to find their way home eventually.

# Karen's blueberry muffins

2 cups plain flour (I use half wholemeal)
3 tsp baking powder
3 tbsp brown sugar (I use muscovado)
1 egg, beaten
¼ cup melted butter
1 cup milk
1 cup frozen blueberries (do not thaw)
2 tbsp caster sugar

Sift together flour and baking powder and mix with brown sugar. Beat together egg, butter and milk, add to dry ingredients and mix to combine. Stir in blueberries. Spoon the mixture into a greased muffin tray and sprinkle with caster sugar. Bake at 180°C for 20–25 minutes. Makes 6 large muffins.

# CHAPTER 4

## Christmas, Karoola

It was a restless night for the steers in the valley but they seemed to settle once the sun hit their backs. While they scoffed on a tractor trail of fresh hay that snaked across the paddock, sparrows and wrens took over the refrain and were gossiping in the rosebush. I watched from the front steps as a dozen or so cars trailed slowly around the corner and up the hill to the church. It must be Sunday. The breeze had just whisked itself up like a soufflé and I felt my skin glowing in the air. I hadn't felt as natural as this for a long time—like the way frost thaws in the morning sun. I felt untrammelled and in tune with something other than my conscious thoughts.

It was a beautiful morning in mid-December. The valley reverberated with the sounds of reaping and gathering (rather than spending and shopping) and, what with waking up and living in shorts, it didn't feel at all like Christmas. In Tasmania, Christmastime is the height of the hay harvest and the valley

49

was busy with tractors cutting, raking and baling hay, beating the rain, some days right into the night.

I lay in the hammock I'd tied underneath a gnarled apricot tree in the back garden and looked to the distance at the hazy lavender outline of Mount Arthur, feeling anxious. Last night, Leigh, one of my oldest friends, had phoned from Sydney to tell me she was coming to visit for Christmas. We'd known each other since our twenties; seen each other single, partnered, broken-up, nearly married, sacked, retrenched, promoted to dizzy heights, then not . . . We'd met up with each other all over the world, in Frankfurt and Hanoi, Sydney and London, Barcelona and New York. Now, we lived a ninety-minute flight from each other and she was glad to see me home. She said she would come a couple of days before Christmas and head back after New Year. I knew our meeting would be different this time; I wanted it to be so but wondered how Leigh would feel and if it would complicate things. I was keen to attract a different destiny and felt the Nuns' House to be my guide.

I tipped myself awkwardly out of the hammock and went back inside the house. I loved the way the newly polished floorboards shone like honey and felt cool beneath bare feet. My brother Jim had mentioned a local man he knew by the name of Dave Flynn. He thought Dave would know someone who could come and bale the long grass in my paddocks. It was thigh-high and scared me to walk through it: what about snakes? I rang Dave and before long he sent his son, Patrick, to check out the hay. As the tractor pulled into the driveway, I watched as Patrick manoeuvred his leg over the steering wheel and jumped down from the cabin. He strode into the first paddock, his back straight as a fence post, and bent down to feel the grass between his fingers. His neck seemed strong and proud where it joined his shoulders like a T-square. He had a way of surveying my land as if it was his, but I didn't mind. His stance, square hands on stocky hips, felt simple and unthreatening. This man knew grass. Patrick called out, 'The grass is ready, I'll be back,' but didn't say when. No such thing as an appointment, or tomorrow at eleven. He'd already climbed into his cabin and was heading slowly back up Pipers River Road as I ran inside to answer the phone.

'Hi, it's Glen. Can I come and visit you?'

Another perfect day a week before Christmas, and I was thinking that it would be nice to get to know Glen better now the floor was done. While I waited for him to arrive I wasn't quite sure what to do with myself. In some ways, I thought, he was one of life's sweet gifts, but in the differences between us, not least our twenty-two-year age gap, I sensed the fact of him would be a challenge.

Glen arrived with the tiniest newborn kitten that he thought I might like, a trembling white Burmese that promptly got lost in the uncleared scrub at the side of the house. As we both got down on our hands and knees to find it, I said thank you but that I didn't really want to be responsible for anything right now. In fact, I couldn't be, and it wouldn't be fair on the kitten. In a way, I realised, the message was as much for him.

We lay in the cool of the lounge talking and listening to music. 'I'll play you one of my favourite songs,' he said. 'I like to really listen to the words.' We listened, in tune but not touching. The phone rang and it was Audrey. Glen took a photo of me on his tiny digital camera while I was talking and I thought his easy confidence was as disarming as his innocence. I wondered, then, if I'd seen his face somewhere before.

'You don't tell me very much about yourself,' he said when I got off the phone.

'You don't ask questions,' I said.

'What should I ask?'

'Well, what do you want to know?'

I liked his way of thinking—his candid and unusual nature—and he possessed a kind of purity and inner strength that deserved attention. I had little or no desire to start a relationship. In the past, relationships with men had not sustained me: they had plateaued, broken down, disappointed or hurt. I, too, had let men down, and wished I could be clearer about what it was I wanted from another person. What I needed now was to establish my own roots in this place. More than anything, in moving here I didn't want to attract the same destiny I had before by grabbing at the first tug on my emotions. I was quite prepared for it to take some time, even for it not to happen at all, just to live simply on my own and sway more like the grass.

In the days leading up to Christmas, I worked hard at settling in, though in a mindful way. Every now and then I'd unpack another box, unwrap its contents, consider them, then find a place for them to live. It wasn't just me I wanted to feel at home; I also wanted every *thing* I owned to have a place where it could be either useful or appreciated. And I wanted to do everything slowly so fresh connections could be made.

By the time Leigh arrived, a couple of days before Christmas, the Nuns' House was ready to welcome its first guest. While my home was calm, I felt agitated. I didn't expect Leigh to arrive at the Nuns' House tooled up for work with a laptop and mobile phone, or to be taking long business calls that seemed fraught, intense and challenging. She was working on a Chinese coproduction that would open the 2006 Shanghai International Festival, but the combination of excitement and high anxiety felt far too close to the life I had determined to leave behind.

In the end, Leigh decided to shorten her stay and return to Sydney before New Year to arrange a hasty trip to China. I was disappointed by the fractured nature of my old friend's visit and felt the need to express my thoughts. Next time she visited, I told her, I wanted her to leave her city shoes at the door, to find instead the peaceful space I wanted the Nuns' House to be. It might have seemed harsh to say these things, and I feared I may have broken up a friendship, but my resolve was firm. I wanted to do the whole living thing slower so that different things might happen.

On her last day, we set out to find the nearest beach, which turned out to be at Lulworth, half an hour's drive away— a simple curve of sand, the perfect length to walk, with no mobile coverage. The day was overcast and windy and the sand scratched at our legs as we walked. We set out at a brisk pace with our heads into the breeze and felt invigorated after making it to the end and back.

'You've found your beach,' said Leigh.

'We found it together,' I replied.

We were in tune in that moment, the thread of our past friendship tugging at us in the stiff breeze on Lulworth Beach. When I dropped Leigh back at Launceston airport I wondered if there might be a divide opening up between us; that what made her feel alive wasn't what was awakening in me here.

The lights shone bright in the valley at the community hall and I could hear the beat of a New Year; there was a live band and the clatter of conversations hung in the air without a breeze. I could almost catch every word as I watched from my veranda and wished myself a happy new year before turning in at two minutes past. As New Year in London was nearly half a day away (Greenwich Mean Time) I didn't feel the need to celebrate the sharpness of midnight in Australia. Meanwhile, Leigh was on a plane headed for Shanghai. Time was just a concept.

Glen rang on New Year's Day. It had been a couple of weeks since we last spoke. The heat of the day was brewing under a cloud-free sky and we decided to head to the nearest big dunes at Beechford, half an hour away, where the ocean beach was empty.

Glen kicked off his thongs, took off his shirt and jeans and raced towards the waves. As he turned around to smile and beckon me in, I noticed his face and torso framed by the ocean and knew where I'd seen him before. One of the books still packed in my London boxes was Germaine Greer's *The Boy*, a book about male beauty. The black-and-white cover image was a version of Glen.

'The male human is beautiful when his cheeks are still smooth, his body hairless, his head full-maned, his eyes clear, his manner shy and his belly flat,' wrote Greer. She could have been describing Glen.

We swam and afterwards found a gentle dip at the top of the dunes, out of the wind, and lined it with our towels. We lay down next to each other, cradled in a bowl of sand, and looked up at the sky. I told him I thought he was ethereal and he asked me what that meant.

'Almost as light as air,' I said. 'Better than beautiful.'

When we got back to the Nuns' House I introduced him to Irish whiskey and Cuban cigarillos. And he introduced me to a version of Australian manhood I liked: a young man capable of respecting a much older woman as if age didn't matter. He showed an ease in my world that I loved.

A few days later, Patrick returned and let himself in the front paddock to cut the hay. I took photographs through the bedroom window of a man on a tractor in my paddock (the novelty of that) and felt like a tourist in my own home. I didn't know how these things worked, but my brother Jim suggested I let Patrick take the bales away as payment, and so that's what we arranged.

55

Those first summer weeks passed and I was kept busy and fit by both house and garden. I bought a mower and learned how mowing teaches you to see a garden; how else would you get to travel over every inch of every contour? I kept a journal and wrote in it whenever I felt inclined. I loved looking out over the fields dotted with cattle and sheep, and tried to learn to call them paddocks. Every now and then I'd feel the need to leave the house, jump in the Jeep and go for a swim. On one of these trips, to Waterhouse Beach, I took a dirt road towards a line of dunes but soon got bogged in the sand. In the heat of the day, I scraped away the sand with my hands and managed to find the space to place some broken tree branches under the tyres. I hopped back behind the wheel, put the Jeep in first gear, and accelerated my way out of the soft sand. *I can get bogged on my own and survive,* I thought; *either that or I'm very lucky.*

My brother Jim had a colleague involved in a four-wheel-drive club and suggested I join up. 'Let's go on their next trip,' I said. So, one Saturday, Jim, his six-year-old son Riley and I joined the four-wheel-drive convoy that started in the holiday town of Bridport. I remembered visiting Croquet Lawn Beach when I was Riley's age, but I had no idea there were strands of ocean beaches away from the rocks and coves of the camping ground. I learned how to let down the tyres on the Jeep and pump them up again, and that I'd need my own compressor to do this. This way driving in sand would not defeat me. The true test of the Jeep was a line of huge sand dunes. Jim and I swapped seats, while Riley prepared himself by hanging on to the handle holds in the back. As we reached the crest of the highest dune, the Jeep became airborne. I turned around to look at Riley, whose face was full of joy.

'Let's do it again! Can we, Dad? Aunty Hilly, let's do it again!'

I thought how important it was to say yes to this feeling, how *not* to tell yourself that you can't. When I got home that day and hosed a ton of sand onto the driveway from underneath the Jeep, it felt as if my soul had also been exfoliated.

That night there was an email from Debs, an old friend and former magazine colleague. She was coming to Australia at Easter and wanted to visit. There was also one from Richard Crabtree. I'd heard about Richard from a woman I'd met back in London the previous summer, at a wedding party at The Duke in Doughty Mews. We got talking because we were both there on our own. When I told her I was looking to move to Tasmania, she told me her English godson had moved there quite some time ago.

'I think he's a bit of a hermit, has a house in the bush,' she said, as she wrote his name and email address on a piece of paper and pressed it into my hand. 'Promise me when you get there that you'll look him up.'

I'd sent him an email, and in his reply he told me he lived in Turners Marsh—just a few kilometres away from the Nuns' House. I remembered my promise to the wedding guest and decided to invite her godson over for a cup of tea.

As it turned out, Richard Crabtree was a winemaker and artist who had moved here more than twenty years ago and built his own house out of rocks on top of a hill overlooking the Tamar Valley. He told me he knew the McCarthys who used to live in my house, and that he'd been here in his role as a volunteer firefighter when the old fire truck was garaged in a shed in the back paddock. He was weathered as well as fit, though somewhat dishevelled, as if he'd just got dressed after a swim in the sea. His choice of shirt was eccentric for a hands-on vigneron: the best Jermyn Street quality in odd colours like chalk-blue and orange stripes, or candyfloss pink, and often double cuffed. I wasn't surprised when he said he found them on the sale table in a menswear store in Launceston.

Richard was always full of useful advice and he took to dropping by regularly for a cuppa and a chat. We talked about everything from local wines to fire hazards, but when he first spotted John Seymour's book on self-sufficiency on my kitchen table, he advised me not to try it.

'Mug's game,' he said. 'I've been there, in Scotland and Cumbria. Ten years in total. You don't have to do everything for yourself. And I wouldn't plant anything now,' he said, noticing the line of nursery pots. 'Just start digging.'

It was Richard who encouraged me to think more seriously about my water supply.

'You have a water tank—oh, and a bore,' he observed. 'Well, you're lucky then. If you run out, get Dave Flynn here. He carts water too.'

I found the long bamboo pole that must have been used by the previous owners to measure the depth of the water in the underground tank, and painted it with blackboard paint so I could see the water line more easily. If the water got any lower, I knew to adjust my usage, to keep washing-up water in the sink for as long as I could, to try not to flush the loo every time, and to shower once a day instead of twice. In readiness for more upcoming visits from far-flung friends, I made a sign for the loo: 'Please be aware that the Nuns' House lives on tankwater, which means we rely on the gods for rain.'

It was good to know there was a Richard just around the corner. I didn't get the sense he was about to invade my privacy; in fact, quite the opposite. Tea without commitment was all I really sought, and that's all I think he could possibly give after a lifetime living alone. I liked how he seemed not to mind if he arrived at the front door only to be turned away if I was busy or wanted to be alone. Other people might have thought I was rude—one of the reasons I chose not to encourage casual visitors—but Richard seemed to understand without flinching.

There were visitors aplenty. Gillian, a new friend, who visited from Sydney, and Wendy, an old friend from London who had helped restore and decorate my flat at Digby Mansions. I liked how their visits coincided, as if the Nuns' House had become a sanctuary for women of a certain age and independent disposition. I'd met Gillian on the Bay of Fires walk. She was a media lawyer whose knowledge of Tasmania was informed by green politics. She'd lived in London, fallen in love with an Italian, but returned to Australia to be close to her family when the future prospects of both the city and the man had faded. Gillian wore wide-brimmed hats and neck scarves to protect her skin from early ageing and I admired her outspoken and singular spirit. Wendy had buckets of that, too. She and her boyfriend, Pete, had been going out for years but were travelling independently this time. Trained as a fine artist, she ran her own business as a tradeswoman in London. The Nuns' House embraced both friends.

On their first night, we lit the fire in the lounge room and drank red wine until we could spill it without minding. The next day Wendy worked out how to use the new whipper-snipper and then showed Gillian and me how to manage it. We took it in turns to slash the long grass under the fence so that we could paint it. I loved friends from afar visiting and enjoyed it when they wanted to help with the jobs that needed doing, as if the Nuns' House spoke to them too. I also looked forward to the day they left, when home was empty again and I could get up without knowing the day might already be scripted.

Not long after that, Sharni, an old London flatmate, arrived from her hometown of Perth with her friend Libby. I loved how she screamed like a girl when she tripped up the front steps to the Nuns' House, and how her being here brought our left-behind London to Karoola. Sharni and Libby were attending an architecture conference in Tasmania and although I was out of their way they stayed for a night with me. That evening Libby offered to cook milk chicken, an old family recipe involving the cooking of chicken breasts in milk—slowly. As Sharni gathered plates and we were deciding where to eat, Libby, whose origins were Italian, said, 'You must have a table in the kitchen—it's where all the best conversations happen.' Her words inspired me; despite the space and opportunity of all the nooks and crannies my home had to offer us, the best place was judged to be as close to the stove as possible, in the kitchen, in Italy the heart of any home. Over supper Sharni told me that she understood the logic of my move back to Tasmania, but had wondered if the reality could ever live up to the dream. Now that she was here, her doubts were eased.

I told her that if it didn't work out I could always do something else or go back. 'It's the beauty of being single,' I said. 'There's no one else to worry about.'

It's not the first time I'd voiced these thoughts. In fact, they had become a kind of crutch, a morning mantra I used on everyone who asked why I'd made, in their eyes, such a drastic move. Sharni and I both knew these words were too simplistic and that going back would be like retracing my steps. When she quizzed me about how I thought I'd earn a living here, I knew she would find my response evasive but I was keen to avoid having conversations about *what on earth I was going to do*. The next morning, I waved them off at the front gate, warmed by the energy of female friends.

I suspect Audrey was nonplussed at the passing parade of visitors I took to meet her, and my hope in doing this was that she would understand how I could live on my own yet not be lonely. Without really planning it, Audrey and I were now catching up more than we ever had since I'd first left home. With Wilf it was different. It was difficult for him to visit the Nuns' House with Sylvia, his companion of the past twenty-five years. Sadly, she had liver cancer, was confined mostly to a wheelchair, and he'd been caring for her for eighteen months.

Whenever I used to visit from London, I'd catch the two of them feeding the birds, or sitting on the back veranda on their garden bench. Before her cancer, Sylvia would jump up and go into the kitchen to make a fresh jug of lemonade, and Wilf would take me on a tour of the garden, remembering to show me the rose I'd apparently given him many Christmases ago. He was so proud to see how it blossomed in the middle of the garden, the gift I'd forgotten I'd given.

As a doctor, he refused to countenance handing Sylvia's care over to another, but it wasn't the best of worlds for him as he learned to cook and clean for both of them and have her wheelchair at the ready. He wouldn't have it any other way.

'The fact is,' Wilf said one day when we were alone, 'Syl's taking an inordinately long time to die.'

I was touched when they shared with me the deal they'd struck with each other. 'If I ask you how you are you must be honest,' said Wilf, addressing his words to Sylvia across the garden table.

'That's right,' said Sylvia, addressing her words to me. 'I have to be honest. He wants me to tell him the truth.'

Wilf and Sylvia managed to make their way out to Karoola once. Sylvia brought a pretty vase she thought I might like, some flowers from their garden, and a copy of a book she no longer needed: Stirling Macoboy's *What Flower Is That?* I didn't mention that Audrey had already given me a copy. Wilf arrived with a bag of fresh lemons picked from a tree in their small backyard, whose prolific growth was encouraged, he said, by his peeing on it.

Everyone who visited the Nuns' House added something to it. Day by day, I became more and more convinced that things were falling into place, like life's own gravity. In this way, the house was becoming a physical manifestation of what happens when you let life come to you, a collage of the efforts of deep and new friends: Gillian, Wendy, Richard, Leigh. Wilf and Sylvia. Glen. I was yet to find a way to earn a living, but I did have a collection of recipes tried and tested.

# Sylvia's homemade lemonade

1 cup lemon juice

1 cup white sugar

2 lemons, sliced

3 cups still or sparkling mineral water

Boil juice and sugar together. Pour over sliced lemon
and chill in refrigerator. When cold, mix with water
and add ice to serve.

# CHAPTER 5

## Autumn, Karoola

Dave Flynn lived a bend or two away from the Nuns' House. His Irish ancestors were among the first settlers who cleared the land and were now buried in the cemetery on the hill. He was a legend in the valley, past retirement age and still employed as a council worker. I saw from my back garden that he'd been slashing the long grass in the church grounds. Now heading back down the hill, he slowed his tractor to chat. There was little eye contact, his face obscured by the shade of his wide-brimmed hat, but I could see that he held a secret smile on his gnarled face.

'This is God's own paradise,' he told me, and I agreed, although I thought to myself our gods were probably different.

Nestling in this valley, with the seasons unfurling between my toes and under my fingernails, I felt a gentle plan unfolding that I couldn't resist. I could see how each year might be the same but different, and that this could neither be questioned nor doubted. I was finding something I could rely on that I hadn't been able to find in the city: a sense of permanence, of continuity. In cities I had pushed and jostled, but in nature I was relaxing and absorbing a more human rhythm. In an article I found in *National Geographic*, science writer Jennifer Ackerman described it as involuntary attention.

> Voluntary attention is like a mental muscle; we exercise it in nearly every aspect of our lives. It dictates how well we think and how we handle ourselves in difficult situations—whether we roll with the punches or fly off the handle. Living in a city with its relentless crush of noise and traffic, conflicts and demands, makes us crabby and impulsive. Being in nature refreshes us by letting us give voluntary attention a rest and allowing us to surrender to involuntary attention: the effortless and often enjoyable noticing of sensory stimuli in our environment. (Jennifer Ackerman, 'Space for the Soul', *National Geographic*, October 2006)

I began to hear the sounds of the outside world more than the thoughts in my own head: even the house seemed to breathe as the corrugated-iron roof cracked and popped, cooling each time the sun passed behind a cloud. Involuntary attention was how I came to appreciate the seasons. Living in the country, ten minutes' drive from the nearest grocer, helped me to find my seasonal senses—the ones that were teaching me to see, smell and taste my own garden rather than drive to the nearest shop. I had neither planted nor cared for the trees that bore me cherries, apricots, plums and apples in abundance, and I wanted to return the favour by looking after them and harvesting what I could.

In following the day—in opening the doors onto the morning sun—I knew there would always be too much to learn. Stepping outside to smell the dew before it dried, and *doing* what needed to be done, every day I felt connected to what turned the world. In a train underground, up stairways and lifts, at desks behind windows, at seats in front of TVs, in meetings in front of whiteboards, little of this was ever seen or appreciated. In those places the source of life went largely unacknowledged. Everyone was too busy. Here I was appreciating how you need time to watch a seed you planted unfurl into life. And time, too, to look after it and care that it lives and offers you something in return. And if things don't survive, there's always tomorrow. The seasons are our tomorrows.

In this way, I came to realise that the progress in the garden was a mirror of the progress in myself. That in getting to know the apple trees, I had come to learn how to look after them: where to prune, at what angle, and at what time of year to act. I only found out these things when I was ready to take them on and not before. If I wanted a border of gardenias, I learned that I couldn't just put them where I wanted them or they would turn up their toes and die. Nature had little tolerance for desire or consumption. First, I had to assess the amount of light, the nature of the soil, and proximity to a water outlet. Once I might have considered looking out over the same veranda view each day boring, but now I knew the details of that view were constantly changing. These February days still held their heat but the sun was travelling lower in the sky and the nights moved in sooner with their coolness. Until then, I'd slept with the veranda doors and all the windows open, but the night breeze beckoned me to shut them.

I kept hearing that song by The Byrds in my head about the seasons and a time for everything . . . We used to sing it at family gatherings, along with 'The Green Green Grass of Home'. I found myself remembering daggy things like that now I was re-encountering my childhood. As kids, our upbringing had been Anglican. We were dressed up in our best clothes and long socks and dropped off at Sunday School in Derby, but in the main, religion was, like politics and sex, one of those subjects to be avoided. I hadn't taken to religion then, and as an adult found I never needed or craved the consolation that faith seemed to offer those who prayed. Tending to the Nuns' House was my version of daily spiritual practice, but this was little consolation when I received a shocking phone call.

Wilf had always taunted us that he would live as long as the Bible said he would: 'three score years and ten'. But it was a terrible blow when Jim called one morning to tell me news that he could hardly speak. Wilf had had a massive heart attack and died in his armchair while doing the crossword. It was Easter Saturday morning, not long after his seventy-third birthday. Sylvia was rugged up in her wheelchair on the veranda when Riley, my nephew, had run in and found Dad slumped forward in his chair. Riley's six short summers couldn't help him to understand why Grandfather wouldn't wake up. I'd been home for three months.

At the time, an old friend was visiting from London. As magazine journalists and editors, Debs and I had soireed in the

same world, even holidayed together in Nice, Deauville, Buda-
pest, Somerset and Paris. She always researched restaurants
meticulously, and as a born gourmand, had made the connection
between sex and food when Nigella Lawson was still writing
about the arts. Debs had been visiting family in Sydney and,
ever the enthusiastic traveller, decided to take in her friend's
new hangout in Karoola for Easter. Both Debs' parents had died
while she was young and I knew she still felt a dreadful sense
of loss, years on. Having just been told the news that Wilf was
dead, I found myself searching for a way of staying connected
to him. 'Where do dead people go?' I asked her. 'Oh, Hil, I'm
still asking myself that question,' she said, mirroring my pain.
Her words weren't comforting because there was no answer, but
it was the best and only thing she could have said.

Wilf had the grace to know that his tomorrows were over
(curiously, he told us so a few weeks before he died). This
didn't make the hurt and shock of his sudden death any easier. I couldn't sleep for days because I thought that he would
die again if I fell asleep and stopped remembering him. When I
went into town I drove while sobbing because I knew I would
never again drop in on Wilf. Everything I did seemed to accen-
tuate the loss. Glen, who had never met my father, offered
consolations but even his kindness didn't touch me. The day
Wilf passed away, Sylvia was taken into a palliative care ward
and three days later she died.

Early autumn has always been my favourite season in Tasmania. On a sunny day you can still feel summer clinging on
like a limpet on a rock, but leaves, made tired by the crispness
in the air, are just starting to lose their grip. Promise and relief

live in air that is as clear as a diamond. The day of Wilf's funeral was just like that. My twin brother Martin had arrived from London, pale and grey from the longest flight. I had always dreaded having to make such a trip—to come home for a death. Meeting him in the airport arrivals lounge, Simon, Jim and I hardly recognised his colourless face as he fell into our group hug and the support of siblings. Although they were estranged as husband and wife, Audrey arrived at Wilf's cremation with a posy of rosemary and roses from her garden and laid them on his coffin, accompanied by the sound of Elgar's Enigma Variations. 'Nimrod' was a familiar piece that Wilf had always wanted played—loudly—at his funeral.

I thought about cancelling the Nuns' House housewarming I had planned but we decided to turn it into a wake for Wilf. Debs had already returned to London, but Leigh had taken her place, arriving from Sydney. We'd hardly spoken since her first visit but she knew Wilf and came out of love. Ian and Ann Parmenter arrived from Margaret River. I'd known them since my early twenties when I dabbled in television in Sydney and remember Ian introducing me to homemade pasta and Baci chocolates. It was lovely to see family friends from our first days in Derby mixing with my new neighbours. Leigh and Karen spent the morning in the kitchen preparing a feast for lunch—for which I was grateful because I had no heart for cooking—and the boys arrived with a new wheelbarrow as a house gift. Martin pushed me into it and wheeled it along the corridors, sending ripples of laughter through the house. Riley wondered why Grandfather didn't have a grave but his other grandfather did. It was a six-year-old's version of the question

I'd asked Debs, the question left unanswered. The only words I could offer him were, 'Some people like to be with the birds and others with the worms.' God knows what he made of that. We played rounders in the garden, and later that night Ian played piano, and we sang out of tune at the top of our lungs. Wilf would have loved it.

The Parmenters stayed on for a few days and wanted to know what I was going to do with the garden and paddocks. We talked about the options. Ann, a keen gardener, suggested a hazelnut grove or a vineyard. She also suggested having a look at what else grew in the area. 'That's how you work it out,' she said helpfully.

'Actually I've been thinking about alpaca,' I said, but not that seriously.

'Oh, *yes!*' enthused Ian. 'Now you're talking. Where do you find alpaca?'

The next day, before breakfast, Ian and I set out on a blind and determined mission to find the local breeder: 'Well, there must be one,' said Ian, ever the optimist.

First stop, the local garage. As the self-styled 'unofficial mayor of Lilydale', Rob was sure to know the whereabouts of a local alpaca breeder. We were both prepared for a fair journey ahead of us but were dumbstruck when Rob said we'd find her two minutes up the road.

We knocked at the old farmstead door to the sound of breakfast plates being cleared. An open-faced couple greeted us, introduced themselves as Jillian and Ian, and were happy to show us the alpacas there and then. They led us past the scampering ducklings and hens fossicking under the big gum

trees in the garden, into the horse paddock and across the soft
fields dotted with white, brown, fawn and black alpacas. The
animals had the most curious eyes: big, brown, direct yet unfo-
cused, and every creature had a name, themed to the year of
their birth. One white alpaca caught my eye.

'That's Porsche,' said Jillian. 'She was born in the year of cars.'

'How do you look after them?' I asked.

'They're the lowest-maintenance animals you can get,'
explained Jillian. 'You just need to make sure they're shorn and
have their nails clipped once a year.'

And that's when I decided. I chose a white one ('that's Safin,
named after the tennis player') and a brown one ('that's Vincent,
for Vincent van Gogh'). I chose them because Ian and I thought

*Jack and Kerouac.*

they seemed like mates. Jillian said she was still weaning them and would deliver them to me in the next few weeks. I decided to rename them Jack and Kerouac, in honour of the author of *On the Road*, because that's where they would be living, and took photos to send to friends. I gave one photo to Audrey, who framed it and placed it on the sideboard alongside photographs of my brothers' children—her grandchildren. I realised if I'd ever really wanted my own children this line-up would have been a terribly poignant moment, but instead it made me laugh. My biological clock might have ticked for a few years but to ignore it seemed more natural than having a baby.

The summer had seen a steady stream of visitors, but when the Parmenters had left I had time to ponder our family's loss. I wanted to return to Wilf's old home and pick a bag of lemons, and even went as far as turning down the street on a number of occasions, but never went further than the front gate. I think I just wanted to be close. Instead, I settled on planting eight lemon trees (would that make it a grove?) with the aim of making limoncello inspired by visits to Venice. I suspect the nuns might secretly have approved of that, too. Audrey and I paced out a curve in the front paddock for two young Eurekas, two Lisbons, two Thornless and two Meyer lemon trees. Audrey called it a smile, so that's what it stayed: a smile of lemons.

When I wasn't in the garden, I spent much of my time scrubbing and painting walls. I started peeling back the timber panelling in the front veranda that had been encased in windows and turned into a classroom. Underneath the internal fibreboard I discovered the original veranda balustrade, painted lime-green. I remembered seeing those brightly coloured painted houses as a child growing up in the seventies. Weatherboards of sky-blue, lime-green, canary-yellow . . . Perhaps I'd even seen this one from the back seat of the Falcon as we drove by on our trip from Derby into town for the weekly shop?

Slowly, the house was revealing its character. When I shared the discovery on the phone with Rob, an architect from Sydney who I'd met on the Bay of Fires walk, he seemed just as excited as me and keen to come and help. The veranda, he said, would be his holiday project. Rob arrived a couple of weeks later in a wagon packed with a surfboard, bicycle—and crowbar. With Glen's help, in no time at all we'd ripped off the panelling and removed all the heavy casement windows to reveal a wide, open veranda. Rob's audaciously named 'Big Veranda Project' had been accomplished in just under two hours. Glen left, and Rob and I went to visit the Red Dragon Nursery on top of Brown Mountain. Rhododendrons grew prolifically in the area, and along with a range of surprisingly exotic trees and shrubs, there seemed to be a whole nursery to choose from here. The nursery-man explained that in the 1920s, the orchardist and nurseryman William Walker had established rhododendrons in his garden at Lalla, not far from Karoola, and it was now a reserve. I chose six rhododendrons for the front of the house, all in blushing pink colours. Rob was amazed at the price—just five dollars a pot.

'They'd be eight times the price in Sydney,' he said.

It had been a productive day, so we drove to Lulworth Beach and swam off the day's exertions. Rob and his wife Sally were keen ocean swimmers, and I watched as he made easy laps of Lulworth. This was what the Australian crawl was made for. When Rob left, he signed a sketch he'd made of the Nuns' House and presented it to me as a souvenir of his holiday.

*Big veranda sketch by Rob Hawkins*

Inspired by the new outlook, Richard Crabtree rang to ask if he could come and paint the view from the Nuns' House. 'You don't need to be there,' he said. 'I'll only need a couple of hours. I start with a sketch.' He let himself in through the side door that used to be the school entrance. I waited eagerly to see the result.

Once the veranda was opened up, the swallows moved in to make a new nest. I watched it being made. Two tiny mates with wings like F-111s swooped in one day to check out the space, coming and going, to-ing and fro-ing, cocky with their dives over several days. The first mud stick was planted on the side, above the study door, in the middle of a single weatherboard, high up but not quite in the corner, six inches or so from the cornice, and maybe the same again from the back veranda wall. What is the mathematics of a nest? And how is it built cement-free without a plan?

I watched the twin birds build it up and up—awkward sticks for bricks, matted twigs and single strands of grass, with mud for mortar, yet as a whole perfectly curved and sturdy. It was home for four eggs that in no time at all turned into four baby swallows, all pink and beaky. And if I stood too close a swooping dart of a bird with a shrill top note would warn me off. One day the chicks had wings enough to fly. They hung around for a while, and made such a home of the veranda that parts of it turned white with their droppings. One liked to sit on the back of the chair next to me while I sipped a cup of tea—it sat near enough to touch, though if I tried it would fly away. So we'd sit there, comfortably not touching, like a long-married couple.

I went to Sydney for a long weekend and when I came back

the welcome swallows had flown. I blamed myself for leaving them; I had a strange feeling of guilt, but Audrey said they would have left anyway. I envied the swallows that knew when to leave and when to return; who knew that the nest was hanging on empty and that it had survived the winter—and if it hadn't they would build another without fuss. They've lived long enough somewhere else to now come home. The season tells them to.

Even though I lived alone, men figured strongly in my life. Audrey called them 'gentlemen callers': the removalist, the electrician specialising in private poles, the paddock slasher, the backhoe specialist, the pump and drains expert, the man from the city council who came to take away the stray dogs . . . All these jobs that hold together a domestic rural life, carried out by men who happen to be extremely knowledgeable about certain things. I might live here on my own, but I couldn't live here without them.

In my recent experience, only a man would have saved me ninety dollars by telling me not to buy the mulcher option on the mower: a piece of string to hold up the back flap would do the job perfectly, provided I wore long pants to protect my legs. Only a man would have fixed the hay-baling machine when it broke down in my back paddock, and brought his sons to load the ute and take away the bales. Only a man could have fixed and sanded these hundred-year-old Tassie eucalyptus floorboards quite so well and known that the ones on the veranda were in such good nick by thinking to look up at them from underneath the house. Only a man would run a backhoe to knock down the brick shed out the back and clear the mounds of rubbish. Only a man would know how to rebuild the fence between me and the next-door farm, and know where to get the fencing and how much it cost per metre. I'm not saying that women won't. Or even that they can't. It's just that in my experience women *don't*.

I enjoyed the can-do attitude of my eldest brother, Simon, who had offered to help build a deck out the back. Despite my obvious lack of building skills, my deal with Simon was that I would be his lackey. I'd used a hammer before, although, as with many practical things in life, I didn't recall ever being taught *how* to use one, let alone properly. They're not sold with instruction leaflets. It's just assumed that if you buy a hammer, you will know how to use it. Simon told me to hold the handle at the end, not halfway up; to position myself far enough away from the nail so the hammer did the work; to avoid crouching over it; to loosen my wrist, and move from the shoulder.

The deck took all day and there were a thousand nails to hit. There was a lot more to using a hammer than I thought. In fact, it helped *not to think*. I knew when I'd hit it right because it seemed to sing. *Don't try to force the nail in with your mind. It's not a question of intellect. It's just you and the hammer, and nothing in between. One . . . two . . . three . . . in!* When it was right, the strikes were all equal, and so, it seemed, the time between them. The sound of a nail going in correctly was like the sound of a

*View from the Nuns' House by Richard Crabtree.*

bottle being poured—sort of hollow and solid in equal measure. The hammer should fall with gravity and not be pushed.

Men, I thought, seemed to know these things just by being men. But I didn't see that as reason enough to want one in my life. The Nuns' House was exactly that in my mind: a sacred place free of partnership where I could rely on my own heart instead of someone else's. My commitment was to look after it, and the motivation, to live where I lived and see what happened. I hadn't exactly taken vows of poverty and chastity, just applied more personal space. And while friends found it challenging—some thought I was living an experiment—I craved the space and time to find out who I was in this beautiful valley.

Richard's painting from the veranda soon emerged,

impressionistic and recklessly golden. I encouraged him to enter it into the local landscape art prize but it wasn't even shortlisted. 'Crabtree,' I told him, 'you are vastly underrated.' It didn't stop him from painting.

I think when you start your life from scratch again you have to be prepared to lose everything you worked for as if it meant nothing or it no longer mattered. The death of my father was an unexpected blow so soon, though, and I felt that my motivation was flagging. I looked at the area of the garden that Wilf had claimed as his and didn't feel moved to touch it. Instead, with my first six months almost up, I decided it was time to look for paid work. I needed a distraction from grieving and would try and work my way back from melancholia.

As if to taunt my grief, the rest of the garden was providing me with amazing abundance: buckets and buckets of apples. It felt wicked eating fruit straight from the tree without first ripping open the plastic. I think there were six different apple trees—one of them, curiously, had two varieties on the same tree: one green and one red. I tried each one to taste the difference and couldn't believe the flavours. Such pleasures for free. I loved the busyness that growing things provided, pondering all the ways of cooking and eating apples, and started by turning the windfalls into apple juice.

Some friends from my early days in Tasmania were keen to see me settle here again, and kindly put me in touch with the head of the ABC's Local Radio network. We met, had a conversation, and before I knew it, I was on air, presenting the afternoon program for two weeks. As a print journalist, live radio had always terrified me: there was no way to control the mistakes, delete a line or go back a page. For me, this was the equivalent of freefalling from a great height. The stress of learning to time your own conversation or an interview to the last second was unspeakable and I couldn't understand how it was done. The penny dropped when the program director training me suggested I stop worrying about sounding foolish.

'No one cares about your nerves,' she said bluntly. 'You are a professional doing a job. It's your vanity that's getting in the way of sounding good.'

There were tears in the toilet but it was the slap in the face I needed. I had to learn how to be myself all over again—on air.

When my two-week cover on Local Radio was up I found I was craving the comfort of old shoes. London was calling, the London of old friends with shared histories and the kind of knowledge that might help stop my grief from turning into despair. I decided to fly back for a few weeks, fit in some freelance work and catch up with friends. Lizzie met me at the airport and it felt that nothing had changed. Her being there was a deep comfort. Later that day, we walked along the towpath like we used to, dodging the cyclists and foraging for elderflowers as we chatted. Lizzie found a recipe for elderflower cordial in one of her books and made a batch. While it chilled, we sat together on the wall in her back garden overlooking the Thames and drank a bottle of rosé in the afternoon sun.

The next day, 7 July 2005, dozens of people were blown up in a bus and on the Tube in central London. The TV images of a double-decker bus with its roof peeled back like a sardine can were appalling and confronting. A couple of days later, I returned to work on the third floor in Shaftesbury Avenue, not far from the horrific scene. It was familiar and automatic, editing features on a celebrity magazine, but my comfort zone was no longer comforting. It felt hypocritical: writing, and therefore somehow caring, about the private details of people's lives who really didn't matter, when the people who did were on the streets outside.

Just before 10 am on 14 July, exactly a week after the bombings, along with the rest of central London I followed my colleagues down the stairwells and onto the footpaths and streets to stop and remember those who had been killed and maimed on their way to work. There was no whistle or siren to start or end. Even the traffic stopped itself. Just one big-city will to spend two minutes in precious silence. So many people gathered together, thinking all at once 'that could have been me . . . '

I loved seeing friends again, making elderflower cordial with Lizzie; seeing Martin, my twin, with colour in his cheeks again as we reminisced over red wine and pasta on Charlotte Street. On my way across Hammersmith Bridge to the underground station, I looked up at my old flat at Digby Mansions and knew that this swallow had flown for good. I had an open return ticket, and after six weeks' away, recharged by friendships, I was ready to return to my first Karoola spring.

# Lizzie's elderflower syrup
### (with acknowledgement to Darina Allen*)

175 g caster sugar
600 ml cold water
6 heads of elderflowers
zest and juice of 2 lemons

Put the sugar and water into a saucepan over a
medium heat and stir until the sugar dissolves. Add
the elderflowers, bring to the boil and simmer for
5 minutes, then remove from the heat and add the
zest and juice of the lemons. Put aside to cool. Cover
and leave to infuse for 24 hours. Strain and bottle.
Dilute as desired. Keep refrigerated.

* Darina Allen, *Ballymaloe Cookery Course*, Kyle Cathie,
London, 2001.

# CHAPTER 6

## Spring, Karoola

I love a broad margin to my life.

Henry David Thoreau

In grade one, we were taught to count in colours using Cuisenaire rods, and to draw a margin in our exercise books using a ruler and a red pen. The width was an inch, exactly ruler-width. I can still smell Mrs Walker's Tabac scent, feel the movement of air behind me as she passed by her pupils hunched over their lift-top wooden desks, guiding our handwriting to stay between the lines. We learned cord cursive letters one by one, and would fill lines, then pages, to perfect them: 'f' was always a favourite, its flowing upward loop going one way, and the other coming down and curling back on itself before kicking out at the end. It always amazed me how handwriting could be so individual, and yet we were all taught using exactly the same style of letter.

Some quality in the joining up, the in between of all the letters, turned them into something unique.

Coming home to Karoola I returned to writing by hand in my book without lines or margins. I loved to find the space to write without knowing what I would say. I wanted the words to come without willing them to, without having to pitch the idea, or structure the story, or fit it into 800 words. Day after day the page was blank but I didn't mind. I was prepared to wait. In London, I lived by appointment. The day consisted of a million and one tiny decisions, mainly based on getting from A to B. Here, I could sit still with the day, and grow with the bulbs without a whisper of ambition or of duty, as I considered how I would honour the things I wanted to and recognise the experiences that mattered most.

The radio woke me with the words 'minus three degrees'. I looked out over the covers and saw the morning valley laid out like a flat white sheet. Through the kitchen window I could see the wrens ice-skating on the old terracotta birdbath. I made a mug of tea and went back to bed to watch the sun rise over the mountain and the colour spilling into the day. Green daffodil tips poked through the grass, blossom had already formed on the apricot trees and the show-pony wattles were brazen in their yellow blossom. At Bardenhagen's, the shop assistant said she thought the daffs were getting earlier each year.

Different things are happening, I felt. The season is waking up and so am I, turning away from an old life so something new can grow. I wondered what I might be missing in letting things happen instead of pushing to be involved, but the desire to lead a simple life doing good things was the strongest urge. I wanted to live by losing track of time, and write words that fell onto the page, words that were neither forced nor choked back.

When I came back from London, Glen rang and I told him the words he had not wanted to hear. I knew in my heart our future wasn't together. If it were, I would have stolen his destiny and made it mine; this thought was too much of a responsibility for me to bear. What about his children-to-be? I wanted to tell him the truth and for him not to waste time on hoping. We've had our time, I said. I knew my words would be devastating but I had to let him go. The year was moving on and it wouldn't be long before I could reflect on my first four seasons at the Nuns' House.

I was pulling on a pair of track pants, getting dressed for an early morning walk, when I heard the dates for the welcome swallows' return being discussed on Local Radio: some said 18 August, others 3 September. I wondered when the swallow family might come back to the Nuns' House and how disappointed I would be if they didn't find their way home. One listener rang to say his swallows had never left and I thought his place must be special.

That day, I'd been invited to a reception at the Launceston broadcast studios to celebrate a big anniversary, along with listeners, colleagues and community organisations. For many, the ABC was the centre of their world and I'd often heard listeners confess to being 'rusted on'. Childhood memories of Derby flooded back, of the ABC lunchtime news echoing through 'Pleasant Banks', the Ransons' farmhouse in Telita. Neita and Doug were family friends who lived a short drive away from us: across the Ringarooma River where we'd watched platypus swimming, and up the narrow winding road that tracked behind the dam first carved out in the nineteenth century for the Briseis tin mine, long gone. As children it was an adventure just to visit them. We'd always stop to check the mail in the oil-can letterbox at the end of their long driveway to save them a trip. Then we'd follow Doug, chasing cows and sheep and riding on his tractor, or stand at the kitchen bench watching Neita bake, waiting for Doug to come in from the paddocks. When he arrived, rolling up his shirtsleeves to wash his hands for lunch, Neita would turn up the radio in time for the ABC news, and place a plate of chops or a man-sized steak on the table. Doug sat down with hands and fingernails scrubbed, smelling of Lux soap. It was always the voice of a male broadcaster that echoed through the house, warm yet authoritative.

I thought I'd have time for a morning walk before driving the twenty-five-minute trip into town. Running up the side of the Nuns' House was a narrow gravel road called Waddles Road, a country lane shared by a handful of rural homes. It crossed a stream and a decommissioned railway track before heading up steeply into the bush. I walked it regularly enough, my goal to make it to the railway track before jogging back home. I would always stop at the railway for a few minutes to catch my breath and take in the view of the mountain, of hills and valleys that filled me with peace and a sense of life being rounded and whole. Fence-lined paddocks were stocked with grunting cattle, a pair of horses snorted and grazed, and birdsong joined in the soundtrack. If I went early enough, the smell of the day and the dew on the roadside scrub and stringy bark was as potent a blend as malt whiskey.

The road itself was lined with an ancient avenue of magnificent gums, some over a hundred feet tall. I compared this new routine, walking under trees older than anyone alive, to my old daily journey home on the no. 74 bus. The route travelled the length of central London's Park Lane, before turning off at Hyde Park Corner up past the Royal Albert Hall, right near Harvey Nichols, up Kensington High Street, past the palace and on home to Hammersmith, where the bus terminated. Park Lane was more of a six-lane highway, lined with century-old London plane trees planted during the Industrial Revolution. In April, their first budding leaves of spring were a welcome gasp for life, especially when six months of winter had been *enough already*. And in summer, the trees' branches were pruned neatly to allow for the height of the double-decker buses.

I thought of this avenue of gums on Waddles Road as the Park Lane of Karoola. One huge gum caught my attention: the largest, it had two trunks joined at the ground. I couldn't say if they were two trees or one, but they had grown respecting one another—separately, but together—sharing the same root system. I wondered how they came to be there and who thought to leave those trees on the side of the track while clearing the bush for farmland. Perhaps they had a vision of it being a front garden for us all?

The reception was open and friendly. A bountiful morning tea was shared and speeches made with modest fanfare and the feeling of a family gathering. I was new to the ritual but felt included. When I got back home that afternoon there was an email from an editor at *Vogue Living* magazine. Could I track down Les Blakebrough for an interview? Les was a master potter based in Hobart who, at seventy-eight, had just been named one of Australia's national living treasures.

I didn't expect work to fly in after being away for most of the winter, but things seemed to be happening with my life without me trying to steer it. I liked the feeling work offered—of being wanted and useful.

Les had also just returned from a break in the UK and was mourning the recent loss of his partner to cancer. He lived a three-hour drive away, in a smart two-storey house overlooking the Derwent River. The door was already wide open when I first arrived, and I expected this was always the case, timed for a visitor's arrival. Straight ahead, through a wall of glass, I could see the platinum river teasing little yachts that tugged on their moorings. Les seemed to jump into view and looked exactly as you might have imagined a living treasure to look, with silver hair, sharp blue eyes, and the energy of someone half his age. He had the handshake of a man trying to save you from falling off a cliff, and the gift of being able to teach without teaching as he sat low over his potter's wheel taming a lump of clay into a perfect bowl with both skill and passion.

After the story was published, we stayed in touch. I looked forward to sharing time with him, sitting by his wall-window gazing over the Derwent, watching its zephyr-teased surface, or listening to the fairy penguins partying in a burrow underneath his veranda. We talked about books and articles we'd read, or the films, exhibitions and artists who had inspired us. In between our visits, I loved receiving his letters, his handwriting all scrawled and inky. A short note with a newspaper clipping: *Couple of little things I saw and thought of you.*

*Something attributed to Clive James and writing: 'polish a phrase until it captures the light' . . . Love Les XX.* Les-isms.

Whenever he visited Karoola, Les would arrive laden with an embarrassment of gifts: a bouquet of exotic black violets from Sally Jo, a friend in Neika who specialised in rare plants; a case of Tamar Valley pinot noir for my paltry cellar; or a smart five-kilo box of plump Tasmanian cherries. On one occasion, he arrived with a handful of echium seeds; he liked the idea of their tall phallic shapes at the Nuns' House. On another, he presented me with a trio of porcelain vases from his own pristine Southern Ice porcelain collection—a porcelain he had spent six years perfecting to rival Limoges. I thought it was too perfect for the Nuns' House but hard to refuse when it came with a handwritten note quoting Theocritus: *Verily great grace may go with a little gift; and precious are all things that come from friends.*

In Paris they call it 'flâneur', in London's East End it's more like 'mooching': to unfold or to discover the day by strolling, loafing, wandering . . . The Nuns' House version was done in the garden with a pair of gloves and secateurs. In the midst of wandering, a branch was lopped or a cutting taken, a path cleared or the odd weed pulled out. Jobs to attend to rather than ones that overtook. They were no duty, just what resulted following unplanned meanders that could occur at any time of the day, often pushing twilight into night. Les called it 'a hand at work'. In this way I fashioned a copse out of scrub, turned a scrubby bank into a garden bed and uncovered a fence line. It's also how Wilf's garden was starting to soften. His earlier advice had come back to me: keep the ground clear underneath shrubs, prune the branches off the ground, the lift will do it good and it's neater that way. The space underneath the trees began to appear and I thought of Wilf's handmade gnomes I'd stuffed in a box in the laundry when he died. I got them out and brushed them down. Some of them were handpainted—in reds, greens and golds—and the lines looked etched with his heart. I'd finally found a home for his oddball family of gnomes in the shade of a canopy I'd made.

One day, Les arrived with a towrope and a chainsaw in the back of his ute. The Nuns' House Hills hoist must have been at least sixty years old, but it was wonky, battered, and missing a few arms like an umbrella in a storm. I'd mentioned to Les I wanted to replace it with one that worked, and this was what he came to do. First, he drove his ute into the back paddock, tied a towrope onto the steel Hills hoist that had been concreted into the ground, and pulled it straight out with the power of the engine.

Next, Les fired up the chainsaw, brandishing it in the style of D'Artagnan with his sword. Within minutes he'd felled and chopped up a stressed-looking cypress on the back fence.

'Les, stop!'

'It's better to chop it down and replace it,' he retorted. 'Really, you don't need to waste time trying to coax them back. Some trees have just had their day. Get rid of it. Plant something else.'

I thought about an exotic frangipani, but it was too cold here for tropical plants, so I settled on a native frangipani tree instead—the flowers looked and smelled just the same, although it was no relation.

I wasn't sure what single thing drove Les to keep going. He just seemed primed at all times. When I baked my favourite Nigel Slater Tarte Tatin, he tried it too, shaping the recipe to make it Les. When I took him to Lulworth Beach we walked all the way to the end and back. I watched as he bent down to scoop up the smallest pebbles from the wet part of the beach. He stood up and faced me, holding out his treasure that he'd cupped in both hands like a gleaming bowl of precious gems, with water dripping through his fingers. Having let go of a man half my age, now I was baffled by the interest of one twice as old: old enough to be my father.

# Les's Tarte Tatin

Granny Smith apples (as many as will fit whole in your pan)
lemon juice (200 ml plus extra for rolling apples in)
1 cup dark muscovado sugar
1 cup demerara sugar
250 g butter
shortcrust or puff pastry (make your favourite recipe or buy
pre-prepared pastry. Les uses Neil Perry's shortcrust recipe)
whipping cream

I have the luxury of a tatin pan but a medium to
large non-stick frying pan is good as well, though
with a metal handle so it can go into a hot oven.

Core and peel the apples. Keep whole. Roll in lemon
juice to stop oxidation.

Into the pan, put one cup of dark muscovado sugar
and one cup of demerara sugar. Add butter and
lemon juice. Lemon gives the caramel sauce an edge.

Cook the ingredients to a thickish dark syrup. Add apples. Roll out cool/cold pastry to a larger circle than diameter of pan. Roll round rolling pin and lay over apples, tucking in pastry to make a double edge up to top of pan. Trim. (Puff pastry can also be used but take care to extend beyond pan because of shrinkage.)

Place in hot oven for about 25 minutes, until pastry is a good colour all over. Remove from oven.

The next stage needs courage and a deft hand. Place a large flat plate/tray bigger than the pan over the tart while hot and then, with a decisive flip of 180 degrees, keeping plate and cooking pan tightly together, tip the tart onto a serving plate/tray. If you get it right—short pastry well cooked, caramelised apples soft but still in round form—it will look stunning.

Serve with soft whipped cream.

# CHAPTER 7

## Winter, Tasmania

The pile of bush rocks that Crabtree had dropped off in his ute was taunting me. They'd been sitting in the driveway ever since I'd mentioned to him in passing that I was thinking of building a dry-stone wall with the rocks I'd collected from the paddock. I was inspired by a book, *Wall* by Andy Goldsworthy, that Les had given me for my birthday. The story intrigued me, of a wall of rocks snaking its way like a serpent through a forest into a lake and then continuing on the other side; the story of a wall unplanned, in sympathy with the landscape, although not expected by its maker to outlast the trees it caressed.

'Your rocks are too small,' Crabtree said. 'You need big ones for the foundation layer.' And that's how they ended up at my front door, too big for me to move on my own. Not wanting to ask anyone to help, I decided to move them where I could instead. Some made it as far as I thought a rockery might work, while others got tipped to their end point at the foot of the front steps to make a rough front path-cum-patio. This happened one evening with the help of a bottle of rosé consumed in between the lifting and positioning. I liked the process of finding a place for each rock not by thinking but by feeling.

Earning a living seemed to progress like this, too. Jobs came in like odd rocks, and somehow they were crafted together to make life work. Over the next few months, while working casually for Local Radio, I found myself helping with a magazine launch for News Limited in Sydney, and as launch editor on a quarterly magazine for small businesses in Tasmania—which is most of them. So many were creative and family-run and revolved around making a living from nature. At a lunch hosted by *Delicious* magazine at Strathlynn restaurant on the Tamar River, a passionate local chef by the name of Daniel Alps celebrated the growers whose produce he was using, and the magazine's food editor described Tasmanian produce as the best in the country. I liked how Daniel seemed to mentor his growers and that he'd invited them to dine, too. I got chatting to a young photographer from Sydney who said he had plans to move to Tasmania and open a restaurant. His name was Luke Burgess. Like Daniel, Luke expressed a real appreciation for produce and wanted to make his life in the place where it grew best. In the meantime, he worked as a food and travel photographer for magazines in Australia. We exchanged numbers and planned to keep in touch.

Freelance journalism is a precarious business, and after nearly a decade freelancing in London I was accustomed to its ebbs and flows. While I was thankful that projects were popping up in Tasmania, I knew this wouldn't always be the case, especially the longer I spent living away from the hub of things. I was partly drawn to the familiarity of work that I'd always done while also trying to open up new horizons by doing what I felt like doing, as opposed to what I thought I should be. This included photographing the sky, flowers and landscapes where I lived; writing and gardening; pottering and pootling. Not really being an expert at any of this, I regarded everything as playing.

I had no compulsion to leave home except on the occasion of work or important events, like Les's Living Treasure exhibition at the Object Gallery in Sydney. Les wanted to introduce me to an old friend of his from the sixties when he used to live in Sydney. Back then Tetsuya was working as a kitchen hand in Surry Hills. Now, Les and I were guests at his Kent Street restaurant, rated among the best in the world. 'Tets' invited us to put our heads around the door of his inner sanctum: a white-marble, stainless-steel and black-glass kitchen. 'It's so easy to clean, you just hose it down!' he said with an infectious grin.

Tetsuya not only wanted us to taste as much as he could place in front of us, but also to see his bar, view his ceramics collection and for me to accept a gift. As we left, Les grabbed my hand and we ran across Kent Street through a wall of Sydney humidity and for no particular reason caught a bus to Circular Quay. On the bus, I opened the bag Tetsuya had given me to find a bottle of his oyster dressing and a jar of black truffle butter. They reminded me of the red stilettos: to be admired on a pedestal as a work of art, not messed about with on a Nuns' House country platter.

The next time I visited Les, *he* cooked. He explained it was how he'd paid for his board when he lived in Watsons Bay in the

1960s. I could see the easy brusqueness of a skilled cook at work as Les chucked prawns into a skillet splashed with homemade chilli oil, followed by spaghettini *al dente* tossed into both. The way Les prepared a meal was the way he lived life: 'light a fire under it' he always said. He was talking about *living*, but his gas-top oven was always more aflame than perhaps it needed to be, and on such occasions, just like a fencer, he parried to turn down the gas knob and to remove the pan from the heat with a tea towel he kept tucked by its corner into his jeans pocket for moments like this.

Les's bookshelves were in the corridor next to the kitchen, and while he cooked I would browse the shelves. I noticed how the poetry and cookery sections were next to one another. Christine Manfield's *Paramount Desserts* always jumped out, with its sleek white edge curved like a plate. I wanted to make the dish on the cover, a mascarpone love heart on a base of berries, because it looked like Tasmania. 'How do you get that shape?' I quizzed Les, who went straight to his store cupboard and found just the thing, the sweetest secret: a white porcelain mould in the shape of a heart. 'Here, take it. *Use it,*' Les insisted.

Over supper we sat next to each other on the same side of the table so we could both see the reflection on the river of the eastern shore lights. I shared my pride with Les in the building of the deck and how I'd learned to use a hammer. Les recalled a Bob Brissenden poem he had in his collection, and went to shuffle through his bookshelf. He pulled out a slim volume, signed by the poet, and leafed through it gently until he found the exact line he wanted: the one about the four elements a potter employs: water, fire, earth and 'his own informing breath'.

I closed my eyes to hear the poet's words as they fell from Les's lips, and realised how much I liked my job again: it opened up a way to meet people, like Les, who few of us get the chance to meet, and I was inspired to find the words to reflect their life's endeavours. I decided to focus my writing on the place I loved and the people who appreciated its natural beauty. I had distanced myself from a crowded life by living in the country, but, unexpectedly, my livelihood was proving to be a way of staying in touch with human endeavour.

I met Christina Sonnemann when I interviewed her for the Afternoon program on ABC Local Radio. She was a harpist who played at soirees in Paris, Prague and Hobart, yet lived in Tunbridge, a bush town in the heart of Tasmania. She brought her harp into the studio and played live to air. She was fresh, young and articulate with long pre-Raphaelite red locks and great natural presence. She played with strength as well as elegance, and sang a range of pieces, from a Doris Day ballad to Celtic hymns. After meeting her, we stayed in touch through our mutual appreciation of words and books. When I read about Tasmanian Living Writers Week, and how the community was encouraged to participate with their own events, I invited Christina to collaborate on a self-styled 'Afternoon of Words and Music'.

I'd experienced my first four seasons in Tasmania, and

'Karoola Seasons', a set of haiku, was the result. Christina interpreted my words for the harp and we decided on the Jansz Wine Room as a venue, in Pipers River not far from the Nuns' House. It premiered in August, before a gathering of nearly a hundred people: 'a huge crowd,' enthused Maxine, the wine room manager, who had arranged generous tasting glasses of Jansz non-vintage sparkling wine for the assembled guests. Audrey was chuffed in hot pink, Jim and Simon stood in the back row, heckling me with their champagne flutes, and Leigh offered the proud eye of an old friend. We hadn't discussed whether she would come. She just did, and brought two friends, Fiona and John, who were visiting her from New York. I felt spoilt as well as thankful that time had let us step through the hoop of awkwardness thrown up on her first visit. It was a treat to hear how Christina had turned my simple words into music for the harp, and how she sensed each season in her clever score.

The Jansz Wine Room was an impressive space. The weatherboard winery was built in the early 1970s in the style of a Dutch barn, and had been a working winery until it was renovated to architectural award standard. It was a perfect blend of old and new, and I thought of it as my local and liked to share it with friends and visitors who came to stay. Some were so impressed they suggested I might like to work there. While sipping on flutes of Mumm and Pierre-Jouët in London bars, or Tesco's Brut Cava at home, it was nowhere near my dreams that one day I'd live in the unofficial Champagne region of the southern hemisphere. I thought I'd found heaven when I heard there were four top Australian sparkling wines in the Pipers River region alone. I tried them all, but it was Jansz that seemed to draw me back by the architecture of the place, the elegance of the wine and, as I soon found out, its winemaker.

Natalie was young, had a fetish for chic shoes, and travelled everywhere with a wired kelpie bitch called Bob. Nat's name was usually followed in conversation by a slight intake of breath: '. . . a *female* winemaker?'

Nat said she could pinpoint exactly when her love affair with wine started, recalling the smell of vintage while cycling through the vineyards in the Barossa Valley where she grew up. I envied the impact that place had on her at such an early age. Through the smell of grapes being harvested she found a destiny many people never find: a lively mind connected to the ground it walked on and a livelihood to match.

I couldn't rely on freelancing alone to pay the bills, so, inspired by friends' advice, I approached Maxine at Jansz about the possibility of casual work. She told me my timing was perfect. I couldn't believe that as a cellar-door hand my day would start by tasting sparkling wine.

The colour itself was everything I liked about a day: like hay or a pale lemon sky, shortbread, oysters or sponge cake mix, or a soft and buttery Armani suit. When I opened a bottle I could smell and taste the yeast. I tried to find the oyster on the palate and the sea spray or rose petal on the nose, and the lingering oak finish. When I popped the cork I loved to see the mist wisp, and curl, then dissipate into thin air like a smoking pistol; I loved how the aroma itself was intoxicating, got right up your nose and lifted you, like a lemon sherbet bomb. More than anything, I loved the story of Champagne itself, of how women had loved it throughout history; in particular, mesdames Lilly Bollinger and

Barbe-Nicole Clicquot, grandes dames who brought bubbles to the world thanks to the early deaths of their husbands. There was talk that corks would one day go from sparkling wine, as they had from wine, but how could you replace the sound a cork made when it popped or how that stopped a conversation?

I learned to explain how *méthode champenoise* sparkling wine was made by adding yeast and sugar to wine; that the yeast ate the sugar, which created the bubbles and the alcohol; and that it was sold in the bottle in which it was made. When women tasted, I watched as they closed their eyes, smiled, and looked pleasantly guilty at the feeling of joy as they sipped, smacked lips and swallowed, but rarely spat. It was a very precise expression I loved to look out for, especially when it seemed a private look happily shared in public. When your job is pouring bubbles, there are few complaints from customers.

While the flock of resident geese was fussing in the Jansz vineyard in Pipers Brook, Nat walked up and down the trellised vines, teasing and tantalising her senses until she knew the time was perfect for picking. Over the bar at the cellar door, while Bob chased a cork around the Wine Room, she explained that her vintage rosé could be from nowhere else other than those one small block of pinot noir vines, planted in the reddest soil on the brow of the hill overlooking Bass Strait. I was happy that working here had connected me to where wine came from, and that it was no longer just a bottle on a shelf.

It was harvest time again in the valley; paddocks were starting to look groomed and were dotted with fat round hay bales.
The lemon trees were covered in exotic-smelling blossom and I
had to stop myself from picking it so that I could take the smell
inside. I started sensing how life here just seemed to flow—
even *swan in*—more easily than it ever did living in the midst
of one of the world's great cities, where rewards were often
hard won. In London I had to push to make things happen;
here, things just seemed to emerge around me, serendipitously,
I think because of where I lived. One day I thought I'd wake up
and wonder what on earth I'd done moving back, but already a
year had passed and, despite my London visit, I'd had not one
creeping doubt. Often I was asked, 'Wow, that must have been
a culture shock, moving from London to Lilydale! Don't you get
lonely?' And I would tell them about how life swans in now,
and about 'deepest darkest Africa' and my uninvited guests.
Listen up . . .

The plumber who came to replumb my toilets invited me
to a New Year party, themed Latino. There would be salsa dancing, he said. Would I be interested in judging the costumes? It
was my first social event in the area and, given the amount of
trouble taken with printed invitations, decorations and planning, I decided to go. I wore the silver Gucci frock I bought
in London and had only worn once for a big launch. When I
arrived at the party, Simon the plumber told me he thought I'd
done well at the op shop, and I didn't correct him. It was here
that I met Paul, a single father who salsaed as poorly as me. We
got chatting and I mentioned that I'd been exploring the area.
He told me about one of his favourite spots from childhood,

not far away, on the north coast. His family had come to know it as 'deepest darkest Africa', when the road to the beach was no more than a horse track. 'It's changed a little since then,' he said. I made a mental note to try to find it.

The turn-off to Bellingham is near Jansz off the Bridport Road, and the road to the coast is signalled by a change of vegetation, made scrubbier by tea-trees. If you go all the way to the end you'll find a beach. The beach itself is long, empty, rugged, and backed by sand dunes.

Thick deep eyelashes of seaweed were strewn across the sand, and fascinating rocky outcrops made fingers into a sea that was wild and answerable to nothing. At one end, I came across a wooden bench: five slats bolted to a metal frame, set in

*The unnamed seat near Bellingham.*

the ground with five big rocks that served as a platform. There was no name, no label, no engraved plaque or signature, just a sturdy bench for everyday enjoyment. It had a sense of gloating in the way it sat facing squarely out to sea in a cove sheltered by she-oaks, tea-trees and boobyalla. 'I'm not going anywhere,' it seemed to be saying. 'I'll be here longer than you.'

I told Paul later that I'd made it to deepest darkest Africa. 'Did you find the bench?' he asked. 'Yes, I found the bench.' 'That's good,' he said, sounding pleased.

Leigh timed her next visit for February, when Sydney was at its stickiest. I hardly gave her time to unpack before suggesting we head to Lulworth. I liked the thought of catching up with her while heading into a breeze on a beach walk we both loved. We kicked off our shoes and scaled the dunes up to the beach, then ran down the other side into the Tiffany-blue surf, expecting to have the place to ourselves. But on this day we noticed there were two other people on our beach—nuisance strangers. We chose to walk in the opposite direction, to the eastern end, and established a cool distance. After two swims, we were forced to head back, nagged off the sand by swarms of march flies. The strangers were nowhere to be seen, until back at the car park we spotted the two men shading themselves in the back of their hired campervan. One was inside reading a novel while the other sat on the tailgate cleaning sand from his toes.

Leigh started a conversation and established that they were friends from Adelaide, had just walked the Walls of Jerusalem, and were filling in a couple of days before, separately, catching the plane and the Bass Strait ferry back home.

'Hey, do you have a paddock we could camp in?' asked one of the strangers.

I told him the address once, without directions, thinking that he wouldn't remember or would never find the way. We said goodbye and made our way home. A short time later, the white van appeared in the Nun's House driveway. Total strangers had come to camp. They told us they called the van 'the deli'. It was stocked with wines and gourmet foods from their Tasmanian travels. Ian told us he worked as a landscape architect and Toby was studying viticulture. Their tastes were refined and their spirits generous as they baked fish for us for dinner that night, mixed jugs of Pimm's crammed with fruits and fresh mint from the garden, and ended the evening brewing coffee with cardamom.

After breakfast the next day, the four of us set off in the windowless Jeep for 'deepest darkest Africa' on the condition they were never to reveal its whereabouts. On a baking afternoon, we stood thigh-deep in a teal-blue ocean with glasses of sparkling wine in our hands. I showed them what I'd come to know as 'my Summer Palace': an old fisherman's shack nuzzled into the dunes with a bed at every window that looked out to sea. Toby offered me his clasped hands to stand on and raised me high enough to peer through the kitchen window.

'What can you see?' he asked enthusiastically from below.

'Well, there's an empty bottle of Jack Daniels lying on the sink, a sauce bottle, knives, a fork . . .'

We sat on the deck and took photographs as if we owned it and I imagined that I already did.

The next morning, Leigh and I said our goodbyes to Ian and Toby and as they turned left out of the driveway onto Pipers River Road we could hear the deli van's horn sound in the distance: the first *beep beep* was a cheerful farewell; the second *beep beep* a sadder refrain; the third, the longest honk, a longing for the moment not to go . . . Toby had signed the Nuns' House guestbook and we opened it to see what he'd written: *If you ever drink from the Zambesi they say you will always go back to taste it again.*

A couple of weeks later I made inquiries about the old shack on Crown land at deepest darkest Africa, but it was too late. The official told me it had just been sold. Out of curiosity I decided to visit it regularly to keep an eye on the changes. The first time I visited, as I walked up the sandy driveway I could see that the deck had been ripped out. There was a hole in a wall—for a new window, perhaps—and some water pipes were lying around. Work in progress . . . When I told Crabtree, he said the new owners must be trying to update the shack to meet council regulations. I just hoped they wouldn't make it posh.

A few weeks later, I turned the point to see that the old fisherman's shack in the sand dune had vanished. I couldn't hold back the tears when I struggled to the top of the dune to see not one sign of it standing. Not even a footprint remained.

*The summer place at 'deepest, darkest Africa'.*

# Natalie's Jansz Tasmania Vintage Rosé jelly with raspberries and rose petals

2 bottles Jansz Vintage Rosé
3 cups caster sugar
2 punnets raspberries
12 sheets gold or titanium-strength leaf gelatin
fresh rose petals

Pour wine into large saucepan with sugar. Bring to boil while stirring.

Add ½ punnet of raspberries. Stir through—simmer for 5 minutes to break down the flavours.

Meanwhile, soak the leaf gelatin in cold water for 2 minutes. Squeeze out gelatin.

Take Jansz raspberry syrup off the heat and stir in the gelatin until completely dissolved. Set aside to cool for 30 minutes.

Pour ¼ of mix into a greased jelly mould. Add ½ punnet of raspberries and sit for 15 minutes. Put

in another ¼ mix. Repeat steps until mould is full
and raspberries are evenly dispersed (save a handful
to scatter over jelly after turning out).

Set for minimum of 4 hours, preferably overnight.

To turn out, dip mould into bowl of hot water—
5 seconds at most. Turn onto platter, surround with
remaining fresh raspberries and serve with fresh
rose petals.

# CHAPTER 8

## *Third summer, Karoola*

The crown of the year is harvest time, and if you cannot
enjoy that you are unlikely to enjoy anything. You sweat
and toil, along with friends and neighbours, to gather in
and make secure the fruit of the year's labours. The work
is hard, hot, sometimes boisterous, always fun, and each
day of it should be rewarded with several pints of home-
brewed beer or chilled homemade wine or cider.

John Seymour, *The New Complete Book of Self-Sufficiency*, 2003

It was my third summer in Karoola and, somewhat to the sur-
prise of friends and family, I never felt lonely or without
purpose. I found companionship with the swallows who had
returned to the front veranda of the Nuns' House and there was
always something to do, to learn, to make or take care of. Jack
and Kerouac were booked in for their first haircut at an alpaca

open day at Jillian and Ian's. I tried to coax them from their paddock into the trailer with a handful of fresh leaves but in the end had to resort to force and recruited four wranglers instead. Simon, Joe and my neighbours Stuart and Rosemary helped me run them into the corner of the paddock and wrestle them to the ground.

'You should make a corral,' said Stuart, who kept a few cattle, 'pen them in. It'll be much easier.'

I could hardly watch as Kerouac was stretched out on a rack on the floor of the barn, screaming as the shearer readied his electric shears. A man from among the onlookers directed me to watch, and I understood then that if I wanted to keep animals, it was my responsibility not to look away. In fact, I could be useful, as he suggested, collecting their fleece from the floor and stuffing it into bags. The man insisted next year I ask the shearer to come to me. 'Less stressful for the animals,' he said.

As well as alpaca duties, there were aunt duties. When Riley and Grace arrived for sleepovers I loved their open hugs and joyful play. Riley liked catching grasshoppers in jars and chasing the alpaca in the paddock. After a while, he worked out that if he stood in the paddock and turned his head away from them, they would slowly approach of their own accord. Grace drew and scribbled and I treasured as works of art the sheets of paper she left behind. Both played dress-ups from the big drawer that I kept especially for their visits, home to all my old has-been London scarves, gloves and handbags—redundant in their splendour. The two of them made a cubbyhouse in the shade under the stand of golden plum trees. Stools, mugs and a teapot made their way outside as furnishings and props. And nine-year-old Riley added the finishing touch by hanging a cardboard sign from one of the trees. On it he'd scrawled 'The Monk's House' in thick black felt pen. I'm not sure if he understood what a monk was, or that I wasn't a nun.

I was starting to make new friends, it so happened, meeting women who ran properties and lived on their own. Libby first introduced herself when she heard a conversation I was having on the radio about where lyrebirds could be found in Tasmania. She knew a local expert and wanted to put me in touch. When we spoke on the phone later Libby told me she'd grown up in Ringarooma and now lived on her own in north Lilydale. I thanked her for the information about the lyrebirds and felt sure our paths would cross again.

A few weeks later she rang me at home. She wanted to introduce me to Annie, a friend of hers who lived just across the hill that I could see from my front veranda. Libby was heading over to see her, why didn't I come too? I liked the neighbourliness of this and that's how our friendship started, over a tour of Annie's garden. She said she'd inherited the 10-hectare property from her late father who was a shearing contractor and kept it stocked with sheep and alpaca. She'd planted a Blackwood grove herself and, in spring, thousands of bobbing daffodils lined the driveway and coloured her garden beds. She even knew all of them by name: 'That's Carnival, there's a Pink Charm, here's Erlicheer, and those jonquils are over!'

Both women were older than me; not that it mattered, because our similarities brought us together. None of us had children and I got the sense that we had learned to look after ourselves because we preferred it that way. They were both lithe and full of life and I liked how, meeting outside of work, we were meeting as ourselves. Job descriptions seemed irrelevant as Annie introduced us to her beloved alpaca, one by one.

'I want more,' she said. 'I just want more.'

It was a Lulworth morning and I decided to invite Annie and Libby. They had their own secret beaches, sacred places where the heart could be replenished, in the hot sand, under a cooling she-oak, or on a cove between the rocks, but I was surprised when they told me they were yet to discover Lulworth.

Libby pulled into the Nuns' House driveway in a handsome vintage automobile, a 1948 Ford Anglia she called 'the old girl'. She looked handsome herself in a jaunty cap and leather backless gloves that fastened at the wrists. The old girl's roof was down and Annie was sprawled across the back seat. 'Come on, Hil!' she called out, as I ran down the front steps. We had all packed cold bottles of beer wrapped up in beach towels and headed down the straight at a feisty fifty miles per hour laughing and hooting like vintage teenagers.

There was nowhere else I wanted to be other than at Lulworth Beach with new friends—swimming, basking, and drinking straight from a beer bottle that had been chilled in the ocean. We returned when the day started cooling and, as we said our goodbyes, the three of us made another date for the following weekend. Over summer we took it in turns to drive to Lulworth, and each time our beach days became more gourmet and basket-laden. We had a sense of coming together, touching base, and making the most of the wonderful seasonal harvest. I liked how summer seemed to heat you on the inside, making you lazy when you needed to be—at the end of the year when tiredness sets in.

It was my fourth Christmas and a perfect morning with not a breath of wind. Debs was visiting again from London, on her second visit to the Nuns' House, and we decided to spend Christmas Day at Lulworth Beach with Libby and Annie. We arrived in convoy, unpacked the cars, and loaded each other up with towels and umbrellas, baskets and cooler bags of food. Bare feet squeaked on hot sand as we climbed up the dunes and stopped to catch our breath at the top. There were synchronised sighs and squeals as we saw the colour of the water and that the tide was just right. Libby returned to the car to fetch a few more things that included a special portable table she had invented. It was called the 'the entertainment table'—a round table top with a pole that screwed into the surface underneath while the other end poked into the sand.

We all brought something for the table. Libby had picked the best fruit from her orchard that morning—a platter laden with raspberries, strawberries and silvanberries. I think you could still spot the dew on the berries. Annie unwrapped fresh Tassie king prawns and dips. I brought a bottle of homemade rhubarb sparkling wine that served as an aperitif, and a generous wedge of gooey White Pearl camembert. And Debs had made a plate of rich chocolate brownies from a recipe she saw and fancied in a magazine on the plane.

It wasn't a family Christmas, or a traditional one with hats and bonbons. But it was a sharing of special friendships in a place where we all felt relaxed.

One weekend, as Annie and I headed home after an afternoon at Lulworth, she mentioned she needed to put away her bales of hay. 'Let's do it,' I said, 'quicker with two,' although I'd never stacked hay before. My last season's harvest was taken away by Patrick Flynn as payment for cutting it. He was working in town now, so I'd have to sort out soon what I was to do with this year's hay.

It was late afternoon on a hot January day when we arrived at Annie's farm; two gold-dusted paddocks were dotted with baled-up rectangles. Annie headed into the house and came out with long-sleeved shirts, gloves and long pants.

'It's to protect us from the hay—stops you itching!' she said. 'You'll need them.'

She introduced me to her neighbour, Darren, who drove the truck, and Davo, who was standing on the back, ready to stack. Annie and I were on foot, loading from the paddock, taking it in turns with each bale, grabbing the bright pink or blue string in a certain place so as not to trap a finger. The heavier bales needed both of us. Working into the evening we found a natural rhythm, bending and lifting, as we snaked our way across the paddock until two truckloads of hay were stacked neatly inside the barn. Annie showed me how to stack safely, crisscrossing each bale neatly so the floor-to-rafters pile was locked safely in place without risk of tipping. She showed me how easy it was to twist an ankle, or fall down a gap between the bales. Finally, we shut the barn door on a hundred and forty-five bales, put away now, all dry for winter.

'Hey, Darren,' said Annie. 'Can you cut Hilary's hay?'

'Won't be able to get to it for a couple of weeks. Try Dave Pinner up the road. He's cuttin' hay this year,' said Darren. 'By the way, you two ladies work harder than most blokes I know.'

'That's high praise coming from Darren,' said Annie, as the blokes headed off. We took time to catch a beer before sundown on Annie's veranda. She went to the kitchen, brought out a plate with two succulent steaks, and lit the barbie. We ate in the setting sun knowing that we'd truly earned it.

Underneath the farm boots and checked flannelette shirts, Annie wore the colours of a master of arts in dance from New York University. During the week she worked as artistic director of Tasmania's only professional dance company. At the weekend, she was a farmer, drove a Massey Ferguson tractor, operated her own chainsaw, and kept a gun to ward off unwanted wildlife. When the local paper interviewed her on her fifty-fourth birthday, she explained her preference for living alone in this way: 'I have had relationships but I'm comfortable being on my own. It allows me the freedom to be who I am and be where I need to be.' I liked the ease of her words and the way they were spoken without the need to defend.

I left for home with a feeling of fullness, exhaustion and reward. This was a life ritual, rather than a day dictated by a TV program guide, the nine-to-five pressures of a working day, or a job that my heart wasn't in.

Since living in Karoola, my shoulders had broadened—literally. An Armani dress I once wore to a posh wedding in Belgium was now at least two inches too tight at the back zipper. I had developed mower shoulders. No need for gym membership here. When I got home, I rang Dave Pinner, an organic seed farmer who lived on his own at the other end of the straight, and arranged for him to cut and bale my paddock. That night I fell straight to sleep.

When Dave arrived a couple of days later I thought he seemed dark and brooding. 'This'll be the last year I'll be hay cutting,' he said. 'It's just not worth my while anymore, especially now the seed business is on its way.'

I asked him if he could just cut and bale it, and said I'd do the rest myself.

'Okay. It's a dollar a bale. How big do you want it?'

'Small enough for me to pick up. You know—woman's size.'

Dave laughed, and I watched him settle into a gentle tractor-sway rhythm across a thick carpet of golden grass, the alpaca frolicking in his hay-wake. I loved the smell and the look of the paddock just before it was cut, and how the wind seemed to turn each blade of grass into an orchestra of light and shade.

The next day, Libby and Annie picked me up to go to Lulworth.

'You've got some stacking to do,' said Libby. 'Looks like you'll need a hand.'

When they dropped me home at the end of the day they insisted on helping me put away the hay. They called me 'the new girl', and I smiled to myself as both of them ran the job as if I were a hired hand.

'Okay, girl,' said Libby, as I started the Jeep with the trailer on the back. 'Go to the bottom of the paddock and work your way back up! We'll stack.'

Within an hour the barn was stacked to the rafters. We counted fifty-six 'woman-sized' bales from my one and a bit paddocks.

'What are you going to do with them?' asked Libby. 'You don't need all that hay.'

'I don't know, but I sure feel good the hay is in.'

Something to do with reaping a surplus . . . If I were a farmer the profit of the summer was right there in my barn: feed for the alpaca, mulch for the fruit trees, hay to sell, or just seats for the garden. I realised I was feeling the kind of satisfaction that makes you stand back and put your hands on your hips.

*Christmas rhubarb sparkling wine at Lulworth Beach.*

# Rhubarb sparkling wine

(first heard on ABC Local Radio spoken
by Sally Wise* and scribbled down)

3 cups chopped rhubarb
3 cups sugar
1 whole lemon, chopped (including rind, seeds, the lot)
150 ml white vinegar
5 L cold water

Roughly chop rhubarb in half-inch lengths. Place
all ingredients in a large food-safe pot, cover loosely
with a clean tea towel and leave for 48 hours.

Strain liquid through a pair of clean stockings into
sterilised bottles. Wait 2 weeks. Chill before opening
and be careful when you do!

* Sally Wise, *A Year in a Bottle*, ABC Books, 2008.

# CHAPTER 9
## *Fourth summer, Karoola*

Australia Day. The sun was perhaps an hour off rising, but the birds were already up. I loved the anticipation of dawn, like a tightly wound spring, holding energy to burn. Kerouac had his neck between two palings and was nosing his way into the next paddock. Proof that the grass was always greener . . . even for alpaca. There was a hint of yellow as the first sunflower planted a few weeks ago showed its face, ready to turn with the day. A family of magpies lined the fence, sweet-gargling as if they'd swallowed an orchestra of flutes. It was a holiday. I couldn't get used to the fact that a whole country could have the day off to be itself together. Today, collectively, even though most people were just making it back from their summer break, everyone stopped, had a barbie, and relaxed. A ute passed by on Pipers River Road with four Australian flags tied to the stainless-steel toolbox on the back . . . *It's only for one day.*

I watched as the morning light finally hit the line of

poplars in the valley and crept up the side of the Karoola community hall; the soft hilltops in the distance were sun-drifted. I could see my slanting shadow on the study door. Hello, sunshine. Thanks to the sun, each day renewed itself, while the night wiped the slate clean. You could rely on that. One day celebrated a happy new year. Each day celebrated a happy new day . . . I tried to carry this silly sense of wonderment with me and not worry too much about the future.

On the radio news, I heard the national supermarkets were dropping the price of milk to one dollar a litre—below the cost of production. Later, a listener called in to ask: 'How could they do that—on Australia Day of all days? How *un*-Australian is that?'

I thought about what this meant for dairy farmers, wondered how they would be able to make ends meet, and how was it possible that milk cost less than bottled water? I recalled an advertisement that had caught my eye while I was researching the history of Karoola in the Launceston library, in the *Launceston Weekly Courier* for 1 July 1920. The ad, placed by FW Heritage & Co.—Merchants and Manufacturers, read: 'We receive all description of farm produce for sale.' But it was the headline that stood out: *We Pay Highest Price for Cream.*

I wanted to live in a world that valued farmers, because without them how would we have enough to eat? I *wanted* to pay the highest price for cream! I didn't phone the radio program, or write a letter, or stew and fume, but I sat with this thought for a while. And then wondered what I should do with the morning. The smell of overnight rain on the garden beckoned like perfume—bottle that, Chanel! So did the bucketful of apricots on the kitchen table that I'd picked from the old tree in the backyard the day before. Maybe I'd make some apricot jam or sauce, or both, before heading off to work to pour bubbles.

Sometimes I've thought (and if I were being cocky I would say *I know*) that when I feel in tune with myself the world seems all joined up and offers up things without me asking for them. On that Australia Day, while thinking about what it meant to be Australian, I fiddled with the radio dial and caught a gravelly voice in conversation. It was a while before I realised it was the all-Australian actor Jack Thompson. He was speaking about an Indigenous foundation he had established, and about a line his own father had written many years ago, a line now etched in his memory:

# They gathered from the living ground their common needs . . .

'The Conqueror' by John Thompson (1907–1968)

'The living ground,' said Jack, 'had sustained the local Indigenous populations for over 40,000 years.' I wrote this sentence down and regarded it as profound. The living ground was ours to share if we cared for it. Would our living ground sustain us for another 40,000 years?

On Australia Day, and on ceremonial occasions around Australia, acknowledgments to Country are made by and for the Aborigines and Torres Strait Islanders. Often this ceremonial prose would seem clunky to me when spoken at a podium, on a stage; out of place. It may not be possible yet, I thought, but in these days of moving towards reconciliation, one day perhaps it would become a universal acknowledgment that we all made to The Land (not *our* land or *their* land) regardless of our race or boundaries. A thank you to the place we lived in and everything it provided for us. Hopefully, too, one that was not duty bound or paid for, but a thank you—heartfelt.

In some ways I wondered if that was what recipes were. If we only reminded ourselves of where they came from, they too could be a thank you to our land, to what is grown and reaped, turned into something by caring hands, and finally handed down through families and to friends in one unbroken line, like Rose's recipe for egg and bacon pie.

Rose was a rural reporter who lived alone in the orchard country of Hillwood, about twenty kilometres west of Karoola. We were about the same age, and as children had attended different schools in the same town, but only met each other later in life through working at the ABC. Home for Rose was an old weatherboard farmstead with a wide veranda on two sides, and an established orchard overlooking the Tamar River. Her driveway was long and lined with bush, and, if I compared it with my own open view from the road, I sometimes envied her privacy.

Rose had many fine attributes, none of which would have made a man feel like she needed him. She could do anything for herself: re-roof, dig garden beds, prune tall trees, make her own cello out of myrtle . . . Rose also specialised in what she called 'veranda food': this meant freshly made pie, or cake, and a platter of plump cheeses, salamis and olives, served with freshly chopped whatever was in season, and, always, a glass of something sparkly. She introduced me to amaranth, chickweed, mulberries and macadamias. It was simple home cooking, based on what was in the garden and the time available to rustle it up. Food with a view and with friends—a form of cooking that went well with what Rose called 'the occurring world'. That is, what was happening *right now*.

Rose laid a cloth on the veranda table and placed a vase of cut lavender on top to stop it from blowing off in the breeze along with just-out-of-the-oven 'Cloud Nine' scones, a bowl of plump berries and a pouring jug of cream.

Stuff, plop, toss, dollop . . . chunks of this and that—I loved the absence of fuss on these occasions. And that if the food were the point of our visits, what might we be missing in our conversation? Food, however, was what we gathered around, sat ourselves near, salivated over and enjoyed. We swapped dishes and plates with each other in the same way we swapped recipes. A plate of food that we'd grown, caught, dug or preserved was just as special as the dishes we'd baked. I brought a rhubarb tart and Rose made the egg and bacon pie she'd learned to make at her mother's knee, the recipe never written down. As the sinking sun leaked into the Tamar River and the first star appeared, we hoped to catch a glimpse of the Comet McNaught and strained our necks to look up at the sky—without luck. It was only 140 million kilometres away from us.

As I turned out of Rose's street that night to make my way home to Karoola, I spotted the incredible tail—a starry smear, like the spray from a hose, that stretched millions of kilometres across the sky. I texted Rose straightaway. 'It's lower in the sky than we thought—south-west and low. Stand on far corner of veranda. Can't miss it.' I wondered how the comet could stay together when its tail was so far apart from its head, but I drove home anyway feeling all joined up.

# Rose's egg and bacon pie

(as told to me by Rose)

༚

6 rashers bacon
2 handfuls leafy greens
3 handfuls chopped parsley
1 handful chopped chives or shallots or spring onions
12 free-range eggs + 1 for glazing pie crust
white pepper
2 sheets ready-made puff pastry

First you need an old enamel pie tin (preferably
square). Line the tin with one sheet of pastry,
loosely covering the sides. Then, place three rashers
of bacon on top of the pastry. I cook the bacon
beforehand but Mum doesn't. I also split the bacon,
half on the bottom and half on the top, unlike Mum.
Sprinkle over leafy greens plucked straight from
the garden, three handfuls (not small amounts)
of parsley, and something from the onion family
(I prefer chives). Break a dozen home-laid eggs from

happy hens into the tin, keeping the yolks whole. Season with white pepper. Then place a puff pastry sheet over the last three rashers of bacon, and cut strips to place around the edge. Trim the edges. Make escape holes and glaze with one egg. Bake in a hot oven (210°C) for half an hour. This is actually two versions of a family recipe put together with a dash of A.C. Irvine and a smattering of Stephanie Alexander—there's no right way.

# CHAPTER 10

## *April, Karoola*

Although the days were shortening, the reality of an early winter didn't stop me from doing things in the garden. I'd been covering on the breakfast shift on Local Radio for a few months which meant setting two alarms for 3.15 am—just in case. Waking at this hour of the day felt unnatural, but the night sky always lit my way on the twenty-five-minute drive into work. Kangaroos and wallabies grazed along the shoulders of Pipers River Road like sentries making safe the way. I was eager to make the most of the daylight and always rushed home after leaving work at 12.30 pm to get back to the house that held my soul together.

I could feel my sense of home developing as the strongest bond and yet, after nearly three years, I was still being asked how I'd coped with 'the culture shock' of moving from London. 'I thought I'd wake up one day and realise that I'd made a terrible mistake,' I'd reply, adding, 'but it hasn't happened yet.' Work, though stimulating, had not been able to seduce me in the way it once had; it wasn't enough to lure me away from the tie of the land. For me, the house, the garden and paddock were all work and pleasure combined. I didn't know if I could earn a living by spending more time at home than elsewhere, but I knew that the peace of mind being home gave me was worth the effort.

The leaves had fallen and the garden was pared down and showing its bones. I never wanted to take the Nuns' House for granted and saw it as my purpose to care for it. Despite the persistent drizzle, I would garden until dark, which arrived as early as five o'clock, and was in bed by 7.30 pm, ready for the 3.15 am wake-up call. I found all manner of things while digging: a perfume bottle, glass marbles, a wooden toy, a huge spanner, steel nails the size of stilettos, a horseshoe near the front gate, plenty of pieces of broken china, and even the remnants of an old stocking I imagined had blown off the clothes line.

When I wasn't scratching and sawing about in the garden, I liked to sit in an old red armchair in front of the wood heater in the heart of the house with piles of gardening books and magazines, imagining what could be done. I was also inspired by a pack of cards I'd bought from the Metropolitan Museum of Art in New York called Nature's pharmacy deck: history and uses of 50 healing plants. On one side of the card was a botanical illustration while the other depicted the plant's history and its contemporary uses. I decided on a kitchen garden as a spring project and consulted my brothers Simon and Jim for landscaping advice. While they argued over its execution I enjoyed the creative tension.

Apart from gardening books, I had no current use for the rest of my collection. My book towers still lined the hallway and picking up a novel was the furthest thing from my mind when there was so much to learn and do. Did you know that limes and lemons ripened in the dead of winter? How would you know this when they're available all year from any supermarket? The old lemon tree I'd inherited in the back garden hadn't fruited since I'd arrived and needed nurturing back to health so I clipped off the dead and straggly bits and gave it a couple of doses of Epsom salts. If Wilf were here he would have peed on it, but Crabtree did the job instead. I found this out one day when he was visiting and suddenly wandered off. When he came back a few minutes later he said he'd felt the call of nature and thought he'd use the backyard citrus. I also read that the first year's fruit on new trees should be taken off to help them establish themselves. That night, I took care to wrap up each of the new lemon trees in the front paddock to protect them from the frost. I used light bird nets that made the small trees droop like used condoms but they came off again at first light.

Sometimes I liked to leave my corner for a day or two so that I could look at life from a distance. I'd take a trip up the coast to Stanley and stay for a night in a small hotel underneath a big volcanic rock called the Nut. The seagulls outside on the pier reminded me of the English seaside and from my room in the attic I could hear the waves crashing onto the beach. I thought of friends on the other side of the world and missed them but also knew they couldn't replace that feeling I had found on my own, of being home.

Overnight, a southerly had been gusting up to a hundred kilo-metres an hour, so relentless that it brought down a tall black wattle at the end of my driveway, blocking one lane on Pipers River Road. I heard it fall, cracking like a volley of bullets on the nightly news. I pulled on a waterproof jacket and braved the horizontal rain to survey the damage. By the time I'd reached the fallen tree, a car stopped and a woman got out. Without speak-ing to each other—the wind was too loud—we began clearing what we could of the tree debris blocking the road. Before long we'd done enough for her to get on her way.

'I'll call the council,' I shouted against the wind. 'At least the road is clear now. Thanks for the hand.'

I fetched the small pruning handsaw Audrey had given me when I told her I was going to buy a chainsaw, and was clear-ing the smaller branches when a truck pulled up in front of me. 'Have you got a chainsaw?' the driver asked.

'No, but the council is on the way,' I explained.

Above the wind that continued to howl, the driver said his name was Hilton and that he used to live in Karoola. He knew the family who once lived in my house, and had played footy on the oval down the road. I wasn't surprised anymore. I felt looked after each day by this house on the corner.

'Hang on,' said Hilton, and walked to the back of his truck. Pulling out a sturdy road brush he started sweeping the road free of broken sticks of wattle. He smiled, I thanked him, and he went on his way again. Before long, another ute had pulled up and a man hopped out.

'Have you got a chainsaw?' he asked me, offering to help clear the big tree from my drive.

'It's okay, I have another access to my driveway at the back, and the council won't be long. Thanks anyway,' I told him as he continued to clear bits of wood from the road.

He returned to his ute and fetched a pair of leather work gloves. 'Here, take these. That'll get it done,' he said, and drove off. I wiped away a tear because I realised that I wasn't alone here, even in the midst of a storm.

An hour later, two men from the council arrived with a chainsaw. One of them asked if I wanted to keep the firewood and even what size I'd like it.

'That's service for you,' I said. 'Small, thank you.'

I left them to it, and within thirty minutes, a neat pile of firewood was stacked at the end of my driveway, waiting for me to wheelbarrow it up to the woodshed. Another job or two to add to my ever-extending list of everything that needed doing about the place. Some things never got crossed off—usually odd jobs but important ones:

Fix fence (it had come off its bolt)
Clean out gutters
Sweep chimney
Turn shed into chicken coop
Move stack of wood to woodshed
Cut down remaining wattles over driveway . . .

When I looked at the list I realised they were jobs I couldn't do on my own. Libby had told me about Paul Broad, a local man she called on to do 'odd jobs', and I decided the time had come to call him. 'Odd jobs' was an inadequate description because, as I found out, he could do most things. His shoulders were just like his surname, and his neck was like ballast, deeply tanned from being outdoors, and straight as a gum tree. He told me he'd trained to be a helicopter pilot until he was diagnosed with diabetes—that scuppered his career. I could tell that it still stung a little as he sat on my veranda at the end of the day, sharing a cold apple cider, his stories and the last of the day's rays.

This was a dying job, said Paul. People didn't do this kind of work anymore and yet he worked every day, was booked up for a year or more. Started work at 5 am some days, and only finished when it was too dark to go on. People talked about time management, he said, but it didn't work like that. He set his prices according to a person's needs and circumstances. He wanted to live in the community and walk down the street knowing he'd done the right thing by the people he met in the post office or at the store. He only wanted what he needed. So I paid him twice the price he quoted for the huge wattle tree that he felled because it was too close to the house.

'You're in credit,' he said.

'But you quoted me too little.'

'You paid me too much,' he retorted.

So I'm in credit. That's how it works.

Each morning, Jon Snow's 'Snowmail' arrived in my inbox at 4 am, as regular as a British milkman. He was the Channel 4 newsreader in the UK whose bright ties were a trademark. Subscribing to his ebullient newspeak was one of the few links I'd kept to my old life, if only to remind myself of some of the reasons I might have left. Stories of a knifing in a northern town . . . a special report on the US election . . . and now economic catastrophe looming. Reading the predictions of financial cataclysm, I wondered, really, what is wealth? Why do we want more money than we need? And why is credit (money you don't have) pushed at people who can't afford to pay it back?

In moving here I'd set myself a challenge: to try to live without credit cards. To me, plastic cards seemed to represent the consumer-driven life I wanted to escape. It wasn't an easy task to live without credit, and almost impossible to book an airline ticket or a hotel without it. Without credit cards I found I had more respect for hard-earned cash and was learning to shop in alternative ways: in someone's old barn, a garage sale or at the tip shop. Weekends were not just for shopping like they were in the city. There were many other things to do with my time and less opportunity to shop here. Instead I 'shopped' at Lulworth Beach for rocks and pebbles, driftwood and sea sponges. These were the things that caught my eye now. I only took what I could carry back up the beach and over the dunes to the Jeep. Everything was free and replaced on the next tide or two. I made wonderful finds, too, in second-hand shops, including a 1940s stole, 1970s glass light shades, and a book published in 1960 called *The Handbook of Crafts*, edited by Griselda Lewis. In it I found an essay called 'Handweaving' by Algernon Gibbs and a passage that summed up, for me, why money and beauty were separate paths:

> A handweaver cannot expect to become a millionaire. He
> must be content to work for the love of the craft, to love
> color and texture, to want to create beautiful things. Anyone

wanting to produce masses of things and to make a great deal of money had better have a factory and be done with it.

There were few splashy displays of material wealth in the area and yet people were not poor here. Their wealth seemed to be defined in different ways: surplus vegetables to swap with a friend, raspberries to sell from the roadside, a vintage car in the garage or shiny horses in the paddock, a garden that looked like a park, and water tanks that stored life. Then there were the woodpiles. While firewood cost around eighty dollars a cubic metre, some homes had fences made of woodpiles so long and winding they circumnavigated the house and almost joined up again, like a centipede sculpture. There were eras of home fires in all that wood. My favourite was on the road to Hobart, at Dysart House in Kempton. The owner had built a woodpile as wide and broad as his paddock, then turned it into a garden wall feature, permanent and decorative with a rose-covered pergola right in the centre.

It seemed to me that woodpile wealth was a lasting prosperity, not wealth for its own sake. It was a welcoming kind of affluence that put value on the future and kept a family and their visitors warm in winter. Most people who had snaking woodpiles also collected their own wood, which meant they were probably quite fit too.

While aspiring to woodpile wealth, I was spending the days writing and gardening; pastimes most people regard as retirement activities, but I hoped would be my livelihood. I had kept up my handwritten journal, but the writing that would earn me a living was patchy, and the garden was not bearing enough fruit to stock a pantry. I felt committed to earning a living without relying on a paycheque at the end of the week, inspired by the people I wrote about who were doing the same. They were artists, designers, artisans, carving a niche of their own, living where they wanted to live, without money being their motivation. This island seemed to be a creative haven where artistic livelihoods were born of being here.

The publisher of the small business magazine I'd helped launch was pleased with how it had been received and asked if I had any ideas for more. An idea had been brewing, so I said I'd work on it and present them with a proposal in a couple of weeks. It would be a food magazine, based and founded in Tasmania, with national and international reach, about growers and provenance. I contacted Luke, the photographer I first met at Daniel Alps' restaurant. Luke was also a chef who had trained with Tetsuya, and had now moved to Tasmania with his girlfriend, Katrina. They'd recently opened a small restaurant south of Hobart called Pecora, specialising in foraged, artisanal and locally sourced food. Luke mentioned that Rodney Dunn, a friend of his from Sydney, had left his position as food editor for *Gourmet Traveller* and was moving to Tasmania with his young family to follow a life in food and to start a cooking school.

'With whatever spare time we have, let's work on it together,' Luke suggested.

I decided to go to Hobart and made a plan to see Les, who cleared his diary and convinced me to stay the night. 'Let's have an adventure,' he said. 'We'll have dinner, then set off early. How would you feel about a dawn departure? I want to show you Tasmania's biggest tree.'

First, I arranged to meet Luke and Rodney. We exchanged ideas for a magazine that we thought could tell how real food started with produce and people. Luke said Tasmanians didn't realise how lucky they were and I agreed. I dreamed of opening a produce hall to celebrate it too. Rodney told how he had just moved into an old schoolhouse in Lachlan with his wife and baby; they were a month into building their cooking-school dream, making smallgoods, buying chooks, researching heirloom vegetables and repairing the dairy.

The next day, Les and I rose early and the drive started slowly. It was foggy on the southern outlet that climbed steeply out of the city. Les had packed a wicker basket with a thermos of tea and the leatherwood-honey Anzac biscuits I'd baked for him the night before. I noticed how he kept the basket sitting on his knees while I drove, and it wasn't long before he poured us both half a mug of hot tea. By the time we arrived at the Arve Road Forest, the fog had cleared, the day was blue and sharp, and the ground crunched underneath our feet, throwing up aftershave scents as we walked up the short track to see 'Big Tree'.

It was impossible to take in its size: at seventeen metres in girth it was too wide to hug, and reaching nearly ninety metres, too tall to see anything but the foot soldiers of branches. Even arching back the neck, yoga-like, you couldn't take in the

vastness of Big Tree and the silent space it had mastered, sur-
viving bushfires, logging and lightning storms. We clung to the
observation deck, Les standing back to catch my response. This
tree had lived for around three hundred years without a mur-
mur; funny how our lives, so small by comparison, demand so
much more of the planet.

That day, tall trees struck me in the same awe-inspiring
way as stars or mountains do; they offer perspective on your
woes. This tree had survived and was being cared for, but we
knew that the logging road that had enabled us to see this one
Big Tree had also carried millions of others out. I despaired at
how these ancient trees might still be being felled in industrial
numbers for corporate profit. We are all hurt when this happens. And yet the line between forestry and conservation was
drawn so sharply on this small island that people who cared

*Leatherwood blossom at Corinna.*

about their natural landscape were called 'greenies' or 'tree hug-gers'. I wondered why the line couldn't be redrawn with greater common sense so that what was here before we came might still be here when we were gone. I wanted to be able to look up at a leatherwood tree in the west-coast rainforests where they grew, to smell their sweet white flowers in summer that attract the bees that make the honey made here and nowhere else.

Luke and Katrina's restaurant, though small and almost as far as it was possible to be from the centre of the restaurant-going world, was getting rave reviews in all the right places, so I decided to take Les there for lunch. He was always keen to see what could be done with produce in the hands of a good chef. 'Let's not order off the menu,' he told Luke. 'We'll leave it to you. Just bring it out!' Lit from within by Les's invitation, Luke did exactly that, and the brisk, wintry afternoon passed as if in a dream, with every dish appearing as finished as a work of art.

# Leatherwood-honey Anzac biscuits*

1 tbsp leatherwood honey
130 g butter
1 cup plain flour
pinch salt
1 cup sugar
1 cup coconut
1 cup rolled oats
6 drops vanilla (optional)
2 tsp bicarbonate of soda
2 tbsp boiling water

Gently melt honey and butter together.

Sift flour and salt. Add sugar, coconut, rolled oats and vanilla.

Dissolve bicarbonate of soda in boiling water.

Combine all ingredients and mix well. Place heaped teaspoons of mixture on a greased baking tray, allowing room for biscuits to flatten and spread during cooking.

Bake in 180°C oven for approximately 10 to 15 minutes. Leave biscuits to rest on tray for a couple of minutes before lifting off to cool.

Eat with a slice of cheddar cheese on top.

---

* Based on a recipe from A.C. Irvine's *Central Cookery Book*, first published in 1930. For a long time, A.C. Irvine's book was the sole text for education in cookery in Tasmanian schools.

# CHAPTER 11

## *Autumn/winter, Tasmania*

I wasn't the kind of gardener who remembered the names of things, who got things right or who studied what needed to be done in meticulous detail. Instead, the garden taught me. I would plant things from seed, cuttings or pots, just shoving them in to see what happened. And I learned to see what was already here, mowing at the right time so that drifts of daisies would appear. In spring, the paddock turned pink with clouds of tiny flowers that Audrey said were ixia. She seemed to drag the name from some place deep inside her brain and it surprised me that she knew. Come summer, the paddock turned pink again with what Libby called naked ladies, otherwise known as the belladonna lily. I thought of them as paddock dames—a force of nature—both beautiful and poisonous. Shooting tall, nude of leaves, just topped with a crown of pink lily flowers, they seemed to accelerate out of a faded paddock as hard as concrete. It seemed the more solid the ground, the faster they would inch up, as pink as a galah's breast or a Paris rose. The Nuns' House deserved a paddock strewn with them.

I wondered how to make the paddock turn pink in autumn and winter, too. This was how my garden grew.

Some of the bulbs I'd planted over the months had come from Libby, who was gradually digging up the exotics and turning her garden back to natives. She grew and harvested native flora to sell to florists as well as to attract the birdlife that she loved. One day, close to winter, I was scratching around in the garden like a chicken when Libby rang, inviting me to visit her for the afternoon: 'Come and have a fifty-cent tour.' I knew that she lived on her own on the other side of Lilydale in the shadow of Mount Arthur, but I'd never ventured up her mountain road. Since living here, I tried to keep to myself and not accept too many social invitations or invite myself to anyone's place. I'd made this opportunity to escape the stickiness of other people for as long as that might last.

I imagined that, in her own way, Libby was doing that, too.

I enjoyed setting off on the fifteen-minute drive, passing the old oval where cars still parked around the edge of the ground on local footy-match days, like a circle of dung beetles. Once out of Lilydale, the asphalt road soon turned into gravel and rose steeply through a patchwork of pastoral land and plantation forests. I always loved that feeling of hitting dirt road, and used to dream of it in England, of the heightened sense of freedom and escape it offered . . . of living on the edges. On the way up to Libby's there were no white lines or concrete gutters, and few signs littering the landscape, as if different rules applied.

At the first gravel corner the Jeep slid and I managed to

correct it without losing control. A wallaby bounced across the road and into the bush, where wattles were just coming into blossom. I reached a fork, a sharp-hooked bend with deep ruts and two, maybe three driveways coming off it. I was confused by the turn in the track, but straight ahead I could see an old Federation house with a pretty rose-covered veranda. A man was playing with a black dog that barked as I got out of the Jeep to ask for directions.

'I think I'm lost,' I called out. 'Looking for Libby's?'

'You're almost there—next house on the right . . . at the end,' he called back. 'Have a nice time!'

Thanking him, I motored off up the bush track to the top of the hill.

Libby must have been waiting for the sound of the car because she was standing at the front gate when I arrived. She waved me into the driveway and closed the gate behind me. A decade older than me, she was a tall and elegant woman with cropped hair and the air of an enthusiastic older sister. Her garden was impressive, like tamed bush. As we strolled through the grounds, she told me how she kept the gate closed to keep out the wildlife, but that she was also parenting orphaned bandicoots that she kept in a fenced-off area. She had an eye for the native birds that flocked to feed on the flowers and fruit of trees and shrubs she grew especially. From the back of her property, facing east, you could see the tops of nearby hills carpeted with plantations: the stripes of uniform colour in different stages of growth, and the scarring of cleared land. Sometimes, she said, the hills were red with flames and smoke when the forestry regeneration burns took place. We turned away and headed back to a netted area: her gated orchard. In summer, she said, there were all manner of shiny berries, fruit and stone fruit, listing trellised pears, nashis, cherries, apricots, peaches and nectarines, and the bloodiest of blood plums.

'Libby, it's a garden of Eden!' I said.

'I covered the orchard because the currawongs didn't want to share the few meagre cherries with me,' she laughed with a modesty that hid the effort it must have taken.

We went inside and Libby opened a bottle of wine and began preparing a cheese platter. I spotted a bird book and a pair of binoculars lying on a side table next to an armchair positioned to take in the westerly views. When she slid back the door of her pantry, I noticed shelves lined from top to bottom with jewel-coloured bottles and jars of preserved fruits, jams, chutneys, pickles and homemade wines. I had pantry envy and tried to feel better by telling myself that I had only been here for three years and four summers. Libby had lived here all her life.

On the western side of the ridge, Libby had positioned a fallen tree for viewing the night sky over Lilydale and as far away as Mount Roland. She called it the sunset seat. This was where we toasted the day and I tasted her homemade pickled walnuts. Libby was worried they might be the wrong side of tart but they seemed just right to me, paired with a crumbly Tassie cheddar and a glass of local sauvignon blanc. I enjoyed the conversation and how the view seemed to absorb our silences without either of us feeling the need to fill them. The evening started to cool so we moved back inside and I was about to set off for home when the phone rang.

'It's Barney,' she said, holding her hand over the receiver. 'My next-door neighbour. Just checking that you found me okay.' She spoke into the phone. 'Yes, Barney, she's still here . . . oh . . . you're on your own?' She turned to me again. 'He wants to know if we'd like to join him for dinner . . .'

'The man with the dog?' I replied. 'Why not? I have no plans.' The evening seemed to be steering me and I went with it.

'Okay,' she told Barney. 'When would you like us? . . . Right, we're on our way.'

We set off on foot down the track and I noticed how the sky had at once lost all its colour but was every colour—almost translucent—like a Turner painting. I thought how when you describe a view it changes so decided not to say to Libby how beautiful I thought the sky was. It just was.

A tall beanpole of a man with a beaming smile welcomed us at his front door and showed us inside, into a lounge room warmed by a huge log fire. He seemed to me the stereotypical Australian: brash, opinionated and at ease with himself, in the country uniform of jeans and a checked flannelette shirt. I looked at his right angles and sharp lines, all rib and cheekbone, and realised he reminded me of Woody, the lanky cowboy doll in *Toy Story*. Perhaps he was the kind of man who could save the day while crying into his dinner plate? Over a glass of 'chardy' he explained how he and his young family had moved to Tasmania four years ago after following a corporate career in Sydney and Melbourne. They'd bought the two-hundred-acre property and were farming hay and olives until he and his wife separated a couple of months ago. It had been amicable, he said, and the property would be on the market soon.

While waiting for the chicken satay sticks to barbecue outside, Barney picked up his electric guitar and played way too well for an audience of two, like Eric Clapton, I thought. He told us that when he was young he played in a band called The Streets, but, nearing fifty now, he played for the joy of it. I noticed his collection of CDs, and he showed me a set that had been sent to him by an old friend called Reg. Each one had its own title and theme; there was 'Fast Music' and 'Slow Music', 'Know Your Roots' and 'Lean-To Music'. I liked the sound of Lean-To music. Each cover had a black-and-white photo of Barney or Reg, and a songlist featuring the who's who of roots and blues: Ry Cooder, David Bromberg, Johnnie Johnson, Leon Redbone . . . Lean-To's cover was a picture of Reg with his arms crossed, leaning against the doorway of an old shack. Barney explained how every now and then Reg would post him a CD a day for a week. Reg must have thought a lot of his old friend to do that.

Later that night, while peering out at the night sky from the Nuns' House front veranda, I thought about the day and how it had moved, how Libby had shared her space and Barney his passions, and how enjoyable the day had been. It seemed to have an energy of its own. A couple of weeks later I decided to invite Barney and Libby to dinner in return, and Crabtree as well so there would be four of us. When I rang Libby she surprised me by saying that Barney was smitten. I hadn't considered the possibility of this and didn't know how I felt, so just told her I travelled slowly these days. But Barney didn't, arriving for dinner unfashionably early, while I was still preparing the fish pie. I asked him to help make the apple crumble topping by slowly rubbing butter into flour with the tips of his fingers.

'I've never done that before,' he said. Unfazed, he washed his hands and put them into the flour and butter and I left him to it. How fussy does a crumble have to be?

While we prepared the meal together, I asked him why he'd left his job at BP and come to Tasmania. He told me how he'd started as a console operator; how after fourteen years, he'd worked his way up the corporate ladder to become the oil company's Australasian marketing manager. His next step would probably take him to Singapore or London, and when he asked himself and his family if that's what they wanted . . . it wasn't.

'It was good you recognised that when you did,' I said, wondering why the marriage hadn't survived the move, although really it was none of my business.

I gave him a tour of the garden while we waited for Libby and Richard to arrive, and he sat in an outside chair to take in the view of my mountain, Mount Arthur, that was his mountain too, and of the valley laid out in front of us. I don't know what made me think of it, but I told him about the outside dining setting that my father had made when we were children, carved out of felled trees, and he said if I wanted to do the same I was welcome to come and get a few big logs that were lying around his property.

Richard arrived with a bottle of his latest vintage pinot noir, followed by Libby with a basket of her surplus produce and a tightly bound bouquet of native flowers and leaves. There was grevillea, waratah, native hop, bluegum leaves shaped like tiny hearts, kangaroo paw and tea-tree. Her mixed bunches sold for just a few dollars each on the driveway at Rob's service station in Lilydale, but as it took all the late nights and early mornings in her life to tend, prune, harvest, trim, bunch and rubber-band them I thought they were worth much more than that.

It was a relaxing evening with comfort food and new friends. And as all of us were early risers the evening was over by 9.30 pm. Barney said he had to get up before dawn to drive the local school bus. Libby had to pick foliage and take it into town. And I'd noticed over the months how Richard never overstayed his welcome, probably because his days were long, tending to the vineyard.

'Let me know when you want to come round for the logs,' said Barney enthusiastically as he left. He might be smitten, but that's not what's happening here, I thought, as I said goodnight and closed the door. Maybe Libby had it wrong?

# Libby's pickled walnuts

young green walnuts (the quantity depends on how many
you want to pickle, or the size of the tree. Use sufficient liquid
to cover walnuts.)
brine solution (¼ cup salt to 2½ cups water)
2 L malt vinegar
250 g brown sugar
60 g peppercorns
30 g allspice

At about Christmas time, harvest young green
walnuts and prick the skins well with a fork to
allow the brine to penetrate. Place in brine solution
for 1 week, stirring occasionally. The walnuts should
remain covered by the brine solution so place a plate
on top of the walnuts to weigh them down.

Drain walnuts and place on trays in the sun until
they turn black and a bit withered.

Prepare a pickle with the malt vinegar, brown sugar,
peppercorns and allspice. Simmer together for about

10 minutes. Cool, strain and pour over walnuts that
have been packed in sterilised jars, and seal.

After about a month enjoy with a tangy Tassie
cheddar cheese.

# CHAPTER 12

## Winter, Karoola

I was happy when Leigh decided to visit again for a winter retreat with Fiona. We hadn't seen each other for a year or so and we both felt it was time for a catch-up. She now understood and respected the need for me to set firm boundaries at the Nuns' House, and I realised how strong that instinct must have been in me in the beginning: enough to risk a significant friendship. Since being here I'd watched newly planted shrubs and trees struggle to take root, and learned to recognise the point when they no longer needed watching over, or to identify when they needed to be replaced with something more suited to that spot. I had come to be able to look at my own circumstances with that same clarity and see how my life had taken root. Now there was less need to guard so fiercely the way I wanted to be.

Fiona was always city-natty, with an asymmetric red bob and a penchant for luscious silk scarves, red lipstick and designer sunglasses. But this holiday, as I gave her the second-hand fur

155

shrug to warm her shoulders, she shared her country Queens-land upbringing and the girl that remained inside. She chopped and carried firewood and volunteered her job was to keep the fire stoked, which she did. Leigh, Fiona and I all seemed to find a way of keeping busy at the Nuns' House without stepping on each other's toes. The nuns, I imagined, might have been impressed by that.

One night, while cooking was steaming up the kitchen windows, Leigh searched through Wilf's old vinyl records for a suitable soundtrack. She tried at least five before finally set-tling on Herb Alpert and the Tijuana Brass. If you lived and exercised in the eighties 'the grapevine' had nothing to do with vineyards. It was an aerobics step that involved a kind of Fred Astaire step-skip, half-star-jump, sideways movement and back again. Soon, Leigh and Fiona were doing the grapevine up and down the corridor to 'Tijuana Taxi' and I nearly wet my pants laughing.

Fiona was enchanted by Jack and Kerouac and called them 'implacable'. I explained how they pooed in the same spot each time, how they sniffed where they pooed last, then pooed just ahead of it, creating a neat poo trail across the paddock. Her Manhattan-sharp marketing brain promptly went into over-drive, developing a new line of fertiliser she called 'A Pack of Paca Poo'.

'What are you going to do with their wool?' asked Fiona.

'I'm going to learn to spin and make scarves and socks, maybe a rug,' I replied, more in hope than anything else.

In the blink of an eye she had invented a new form of lit-erature, dubbing it 'knit lit'. It would be the next thing after 'chick lit': stories about love and life learned from people meeting together to knit.

I loved how Leigh shared her friendships and made us family; we didn't need to knit. After they left for Sydney and New York, I lay in the hammock on the front veranda with a cigarillo and whiskey. While the local frog orchestra was tuning up for the evening performance, I felt cocooned by the gentle sway of the netting and knew then that Leigh and Fiona would probably be back before I returned their visits. The sound of a car door banging shut in the driveway startled me, and there was a call at the front door. A stranger introduced himself.

'Hi, I'm Paul, I live at Treetops, just round the corner in Karoola Road.' He told me he'd moved here from Sydney, was thinking of getting alpaca and had noticed the two in my front paddock. 'Do you mind if I ask you, what are they like to keep?'

'They're the lowest-maintenance animals on the planet,' I said, recalling Jillian's words.

He was interested in the fleece so I showed him the bags of wool I had stored in one corner of my spare room and the spinning wheel I'd found in an op shop in another.

'I just need to learn how to put the two together . . .'

'You need my friend Vita,' he said, scrawling a phone number onto a scrap of paper. 'Make sure you call.'

I phoned Vita the next morning. 'Can you come today?' she said in such a way that I felt it would be rude to refuse. 'Don't forget to bring your wheel.'

Vita was a transsexual in her seventies who lived on her own in an old cottage in Launceston with a veranda that fronted the street. The front door was wide open and welcoming, and the corridor was lined with paintings leaning against the wall. There were portraits of ethereal-looking women, including one, she explained, of her late wife. She was dressed in men's clothing, a cardigan and trousers, but her nails were long and there was a hint of mascara or eyeliner around her eyes. Vita gestured for me to bring my spinning wheel inside. I set it down in the sunlit hall, just inside the open front door.

'Right, there are a few things we need to do first,' she explained. 'The wheel must be oiled and taken care of.'

She leaned forward over the wheel and started wiping it down right there and then as if it were an old friend, oiling the joints and moving parts carefully with a swipe or two of Vaseline. I'd been told I should learn to spin with sheep's fleece as it was easier to handle and not as fine as alpaca.

'If alpaca is what you will be using, then why not learn with it?' said Vita. 'You won't know any different.'

Then, with the fleece between her thumb and fingers, in one graceful, flowing, mesmeric movement she turned the wheel, guided the ginger strands, and spun the fleece that had been sheared off Jack's back.

'So many people pump the wheel,' she said, 'but it's not necessary. You need to be calm and smooth and slow, like this . . .'

I loved the moment that seemed spun itself, the light spilling through the front door onto the wheel that turned under Vita's delicate touch. When it was my turn we swapped seats and I started by getting the measure of the pedal. It seemed the trick was to find a rhythm, to move the wheel at a speed that required the least intervention from the spinner. Vita watched without teaching and that was a lesson in itself; simply her presence was enough to still me. Eventually, some of the fleece I'd seen grow fluffy on alpaca backs in the paddock had turned to soft wisps of wool in my fingers. Vita let me find my own way and said the rest was practice.

I stayed for a couple of hours, then thanked her, leaving her with the rest of the bag of fleece as well as some blueberry muffins I'd baked that morning. When I got home there was already a message from Vita on the answerphone. 'Come back when you can. I'll have some balls of your wool for you.'

'Darling,' emailed Fiona when I told her I'd been taught how to spin by a transsexual. 'Whoever said Tasmania was dull hadn't been to your place . . . Somehow it makes absolute sense that a transsexual should know how to handle alpaca fleece. If you think about it, the animals are quite transsexual themselves with those long luscious eyelashes and come-hither looks.'

A couple of weeks had passed since I'd talked to Barney about fetching the logs from his property, so I rang him and arranged a time to meet the following day. He was packing up the farm and getting it ready to sell, so was happy to take a break and show me around, to the river first, the rainforest with its fairy glade, and the old train carriage set in the bush not going anywhere. In doing this, he was also saying goodbye to the things he had loved the most, the tree lines he had planted, the romance he had shared with this landscape. Yet, he showed no sign of regret. He knew how to survive. The logs, he said, were in the valley. Would I like to drive the tractor to collect them?

'I've never driven a tractor before,' I said, a little startled.

'I'll show you,' he said.

'I'm not really dressed for a tractor.'

'Doesn't matter.'

It was liberating that it didn't matter that I didn't know and I felt struck. I liked how we both seemed open to doing things when they needed doing, recalling the way he just got on with rubbing butter into flour to make the crumble when he'd never done it before. I hopped into the seat of the old Massey Ferguson, noticing how it was shaped to fit the driver's bottom. I remembered how Doug's tractor at the farm in Telita had a seat just like that and, again, childhood memories came flooding back: the smell of the pig farm; Doug's dogs barking, tied to their chains; kids laughing in the hay barn; Neita's perfect rose blooms and dahlia borders and her pavlovas smothered in bananas and cream . . . memories all revisited in the space of this tractor moment. Barney showed me the gears: 'That's first, and here's reverse.' As we started chugging up the bush track, I gripped Miss Fergie's steering wheel and turned to look over my shoulder. Barney's face seemed to have no angles now— instead it was stretched soft with the warmest of smiles. There's every chance, I thought, that how I'm seeing him is how I'm feeling . . .

'You'll have to come over for a Barn curry!' he said as I left with the logs.

'Yes, I'd like that.'

A few weeks later, Barney rang to invite me over for dinner that evening. I liked that it was tonight and not next week;
I still felt reluctant to start a relationship, and couldn't be sure
that this was even likely to happen with Barn. But without the
expectation of a date planned in advance it felt natural to say
yes. By now it was spring and daffodils lined the bend where
I'd lost my way some weeks before. Their tight buds continued
to appear all the way up the potholed gravel driveway to his
house and almost as far as the front door. The air felt cooler at
this altitude, the last light lingered over the horizon, and there
wasn't a breath of wind.

We sat outside on the front veranda to watch the sun setting through the cherry tree in the foreground and over the
Pipers River valley. The sky was the colour of a peace rose—all
lemony and pink—and wispy strands of clouds teased us with
their transitory shapes: *That's a herringbone . . . look, now it's
a galloping dragon, can you see? No, it's a dolphin diving in cir-
cles . . .* Nature had wrapped us in her embrace and seemed to
cast a spell when I leaned over and kissed Barney on the lips.
I think I surprised myself just as much as him, as the kiss had
come from nowhere either conscious or expected. The sunset
still held our attention and, despite the kiss, or maybe because
of it, we decided to move higher to catch every last drop of setting sun. We drove to the top of his mountain property with a
bottle of wine and two half-filled glasses. It didn't matter that
they spilled as we hit the bumpy track in his four-wheel drive
to take in the view of the north coast at sunset. We drove right
to the top of the hill that Barney called Bill Hill, a vast expanse

of sloping-away paddock with a view to the sea. I decided to get out and walk, while Barney followed in his vehicle.

We returned to the house and while Barney cooked a chicken curry from scratch I browsed through his bookshelf. In between the motorbike and management texts, I found a doorstopper called *Funk & Wagnalls' Standard Dictionary of the English Language*, and spotted a couple of old women's weekly magazines from the days when they cost nine pence. It was fun to check our stars for the week when neither of us was born: Barney's sign, Pisces, read, 'You've begun a cycle which is to shape and colour the next twelve to twenty-five years. If you have that much time. A few potholes on the way.' Mine, Sagittarius, said, 'Slowly you are building up a new circle of friends. This week brings a man of unusual personality into your group. Be careful how you handle this association.' Barney laughed while I raised an eyebrow at the aptness of the words that also held the possibility of wounds.

The curry was good, hearty, and burned-orange-spiced with turmeric and paprika, cinnamon sticks and pods of cardamom. Afterwards, we kissed again and it seemed to come from somewhere deep inside of us, unspoken and unconscious. It was an old *Cosmo* relationship story: 'How to get from the couch to the bed'. But none of that advice came to mind at all. Much later, when we sat talking on his bed with our backs against the headboard, I couldn't even recall how we did. Barn pulled out his old photo albums and as he turned the pages I saw a typical Aussie boy at the beach, camping, with cars, with mates, with dogs, with girls, with guitars, with a Ducati in his front lounge . . . It was obvious that he'd been a bit of a rogue, confirmed when he told me that he hadn't finished high school. The childhood images left a more sensitive impression which interested me: close-ups he'd taken of beautiful flowers, with his pets, and of glorious sunsets. He told me he'd spent his twenties doing odd jobs, driving trucks, delivering swimming pools, working on his parents' citrus farm, travelling through Europe in a second-hand Jaguar, and running a fruit stall on the outskirts of Gosford. I liked the breadth of a six-foot-three tall man who started driving a Ford Thames and went on to race Ducatis.

Behind the Aussie bravado, I saw a sensitive soul who appreciated natural beauty and was open to sharing it. He turned to a photo of a much wider-girthed oil company man. 'I don't think I would have liked you then,' I said, thinking of the *Cosmo* girl studying her feminist texts, quickly adding, 'You probably wouldn't have liked me either.'

When I left early the next morning, Barney kneeled at the front gate with one arm draped over his black dog, Harry, and they saw me off together. I wiped the dew from inside the windscreen so that I could see to drive home down the steep misty mountain track, the sun just rising behind me. As the road levelled off at the bottom I felt the same sense of peace I'd felt on Bill Hill the previous night. If it felt this peaceful *with* someone, I thought, then why wouldn't I want it?

*I feel like melting bubbles*, I texted Barney later that day. *I want to permanently melt you, not only when we kiss*, he texted back. And I gasped and smiled and melted all at once. When he asked me if that meant we were going out, 'like boyfriend and girlfriend', I found myself saying, reluctantly yet truthfully, 'Yes . . . yes, it does.'

# Barn's chicken curry
## (adapted from Charmaine Solomon*)

1.5 kg chicken breast

3 tbsp ghee or oil

¼ tsp fenugreek seeds

10 curry leaves

2 large onions, chopped

4 cloves garlic, crushed

2 tsp fresh ginger

1 tsp turmeric

1 tsp chilli powder

1 tbsp ground coriander

1 tsp ground cumin

½ tsp ground fennel

2 tsp paprika

2 tsp salt

2 tbsp white vinegar

2 tins diced tomatoes

8 cardamom pods, bruised

1 cinnamon stick

1 large tin coconut cream

Cube the chicken.

Heat the ghee and fry the fenugreek and curry leaves with onion, garlic and ginger until soft and golden. Turn off the heat.

Add turmeric, chilli, coriander, cumin, fennel, paprika and salt.

Turn heat on, add white vinegar, stir well.

Add the chicken. Stir to mix in the spices over a medium heat until chicken is two-thirds cooked.

Add tomatoes, cardamom pods and cinnamon stick and cook for 20 minutes.

Add coconut cream. Taste and add more salt or a sprinkle of sugar if desired.

Serve with rice and poppadums.

* Charmaine Solomon, *The Complete Asian Cookbook*, Weldon Publishing, Sydney, 1992.

# CHAPTER 13

## *Fifth summer, Karoola*

I loved the sounds that drifted across the valley to the hammock on the front veranda. Cattle moaning reverberated up and down the straight and into the distance, and the birdsong in the background was loud and insistent. I pondered how, for a very long time, change had been a constant in my life. Now, it was constancy that moved me; the ritual of waking and moving, like a sunflower, with the day, and of being nourished by one place.

Sadly, the food magazine I'd been working on for some weeks with Luke and Rodney did not eventuate. Instead I thought about setting up a produce hall and was inspired one day when I took a shortcut to Lulworth Beach down School Road. It was a winding country lane, lined on both sides by a red-leafed hedgerow, interrupted by two buildings of note. A sturdy weatherboard hall sat halfway down on the right-hand side next to a picturesque white weatherboard Anglican church. On the front of the dark-green hall was a sign that read '1936 Coronation Hall'. It was built by the Pipers River community in commemoration of the coronation of Britain's King George VI. Sadly, it now stood derelict, its windows and doors boarded up. To the left of the front door was a raised ticket window. I imagined the men arriving in their smartish hats, and ladies in glamorous stoles, and the ticket-checker peering through the window on the lookout for outsiders, interlopers, or youngsters trying to sneak through for free. Around the back, though, was a window, high up, with one windowpane missing. I found a couple of bricks to stand on among the bracken and the blackberries, and hoisted myself up to peer inside. It looked as though it might once have been the kitchen. Rats'

*Coronation Hall, School Road, Pipers River.*

and birds' nests festooned the place, and the floor was splattered with layers of droppings, hay and abandonment. But there was something about this building that attracted me, and I was filled with a sense of possibility. Outside, I found a small placard in the front yard displaying a typed letter on local council letterhead. The building had been declared derelict and was to be demolished. It would make a great produce hall, I thought.

Leigh was on sabbatical from her job and offered to help bring this vision to life. I invited her to come and stay for a few weeks' retreat and to play more with the idea. Together we produced a proposal for a food magazine, produce hall and market. Barney said he thought the hall was too isolated to make it work, but Libby and Richard agreed it was worth a go and contributed their ideas. We presented our plan to the council, who seemed interested, although not to the point of committing funds. A lack of funds, after all, was why they wanted to knock the hall down—they couldn't afford its upkeep. Why maintain a building that was neglected, was the view of its aldermen and women. The answer, I thought, was simple. Because it was the community who built it, it was ours . . .

Between us, Leigh and I managed to convince one or two potential investors to commit some funds. And we hoped it might be enough, although the profits were not likely to show for some time to come. During this time, Leigh got to know Barney. He wasn't the kind of person to want to spend hours in our conversations, nor did we expect him to, but she liked how much we seemed to light up in each other's company and wanted to see it work.

Barney and I were several months into our relationship

when the house across the road came up for sale. He'd been looking for a new home for nearly six months without much luck, and I rang him with the details. He viewed the house that day and decided it had what he needed. Within the month, he'd moved in and was celebrating his first Christmas alone with his three children, Rachael, James and Billy. I knew the sense of space I'd been mindful to create would be altered and that a new space must somehow work itself out. Barn was concerned how he and his family would impact on me but it was a question neither of us could answer.

'If it's the right house for you, you should buy it,' I told him. 'We're big kids, we'll work it out.'

I knew that living across the road from the man I was seeing, in a place that I thought of as my own private corner, was going to be a balancing act. It was through keeping my own company that I had awoken to new pleasures in this place, and they were still fresh shoots. But the newer shoots of an unexpected relationship seemed welcome too. Leigh advised me not to push Barney away. 'Give it at least four seasons,' she said. 'He obviously adores you.'

After six weeks Leigh returned to Sydney. We both remained hopeful that the produce hall might happen but didn't want to push it; it would find its time. Barney had been patient and I suspected he was relieved to see Leigh leave because his love rushed in like a king tide. One day I came home to find a huge heart made of freshly picked rose petals arranged at my back door. I left it there for days to watch the petals dry and scatter on the wind.

'You are perfect,' he said. 'No, I am not perfect,' I replied.

I know that I'm not. 'But you are perfect for me,' he decided. And that's how we grew.

Audrey saw the remains of the petal heart on the deck and said it was an unusual thing for a man to do. I wasn't sure if there was a warning in her words but thought he was just primed for love.

On the outside, Barney seemed on top of the separation, but the proud man and father was also dealing with the unravelling of his life and that could not have been easy. Some days he stayed with me, or I with him. And then there were days when his children were with him and I had space. On these days, he waved from his paddock at 'my sweet lady writer in the window'. Or we met on a seat in the paddock in between our homes and shared a glass of wine. Or caught each other late at night when the children were in bed; a hug goodnight, words whispered, assurances made that we were in each other's hearts. Some days it was harder to leave than others and on these occasions, I walked Barney home and he turned straight around and walked me back. Between us we made a path across the paddock which became well trodden as it threaded itself around the apple trees like an alpaca track.

By this time it was late summer, Dave Pinner had baled the paddock again and I needed to drop in the cash I owed him. The price had gone up from one dollar a bale to a dollar fifty and there were only thirty-five bales this year because the smaller front paddock had been turned into lawn by Barney's mowing. It hardly seemed worth Dave's effort but he came anyway, regular as the season. Dave was a man whose old barns were all in use. He'd been an organic farmer for fifteen years, making a living on 200 acres growing tomatoes, spelt, oats, corn, peas and beans for the seed market. His farm was certified organic through a rigorous accreditation program developed by the Tasmanian Organic-Dynamic Producers association. Dave was working at the cutting edge of sustainable agriculture but hadn't moved here with dreams from elsewhere. In fact, he said he was born in the house right across the road from where he now lived.

Dave wasn't at home when I called in but a woman with a

warm and friendly face and bright intelligent eyes greeted me at the front door.

'Hi, I'm Lyndy. I'm working . . . well, living here now.'

Lyndy went on to explain that she was helping Dave with his seed business until one day she looked at him across the paddock and realised, in a lightbulb moment, what fantastic legs he had. She blamed the heifers that were carrying on in the background. When Dave explained to her that the heifer was noisy because she was somewhat frustrated, Lyndy replied, 'I know how she feels!' And, apparently, that was that . . . Now she and Dave shared the same room and woke up every morning with a hug.

Lyndy loved to chat; in fact, most country people enjoyed a conversation over tea and a plate. Although always busy, they were never busy in the way city people were—where lunch was often skipped, or eaten at the computer, and care and conversations were both truncated. You needed time in the country, time enough to discuss the weather and ask, 'How are you going?' or 'How's the family?'

Before I knew it, it was shearing season again and still the corral had not been built. This time I recruited Annie's experienced handling. It was baking hot at 9 am, but somehow we succeeded in wrangling the alpacas and Annie's natural courage helped. *It's got to be easier than this*, I thought. We each secured a rope around an alpaca's neck, and were both lying, chatting, in the long grass of the paddock under the hot sun, Annie with her leg over Jack and me with Kerouac frothing at the tautness of the rope, when Ian the shearer drove up the driveway.

'You need to get them used to the lead,' he said. 'Practise putting it on and walking them once a week so they get used to it.'

I knew that alpaca would do this because there was a man who turned up in the Launceston mall with his perfectly tamed alpaca. Taming was not for me, though. I preferred to admire them from a distance and to know that they were happy. I told myself that at least this only had to happen once a year and hopefully they wouldn't hate me for it.

When his children were with their mother, Barney and I were always busy, although never with ready-made plans, and I found that our love grew by doing things together. Barn would throw a chainsaw in the back of the ute, followed by his dog Harry, and off we'd go to collect and split firewood from the bush. Or we'd get in the car, find a gravel road we hadn't been up, slide around the corners, stop to pick wildflowers or forage for wild blackberries and breathe in the day. After I'd interviewed one of Australia's top rosarians for the radio, we decided to visit her garden in Elizabeth Town.

We arrived at Forest Hall to find Susan Irvine under a wide-brimmed hat, casting sharp shadows as she made busy tracks on her ride-on mower. With the grace and courtesy of a bygone era, Susan took time out in the heat of the day to walk us—not in a meandering way—through her magnificent garden. Among its many virtues I loved the way it rambled, although in an organised way, and how she left many roses deliberately unpruned. The pergola and crabapple walks fringed with mauve-flowering catmint were architectural delights—you could tell she loved to share them, no matter how often.

'My mother would love your garden,' I told Susan.

It was midday-hot and not a day for lingering, so Susan encouraged us to travel further afield, twenty minutes' drive away, to Wychwood, where she said her friends Peter and Karen had created a magical garden and nursery. She was sure they'd be happy for us to take a picnic and sit in the shade by the river to enjoy the day. As we were leaving, Susan asked if we'd like to dig up one or two small trees that had self-seeded under the graceful oak that shaded the driveway. We looked at each other and shared the answer with our eyes. 'No, thank you,' Barn said, 'not today, we'll come again if that's okay.'

'Come back, and bring your mother next time!' Susan urged as we waved goodbye.

We made our way to Wychwood in Mole Creek and did exactly as Susan suggested. Peter met us at the front gate and asked if we'd like a tour or to find our own way around. We decided to wander through the colourful arching beds, a labyrinth made of mown grass, and silver birch copses shading families of red-and-white toadstools. We continued down to the river where frogs and river birds played, and took off our shoes and socks to feel the sun on our feet and the fresh mountain water between our toes.

Wychwood charmed us. We left with a few nursery plants and a gift we asked Peter to choose for us that we could leave with Susan on our way home by way of thanks. He chose a rare variety of clematis that he knew she didn't have, and refused to let us pay him for it. 'No, it's a gift for Susan,' he said. As we left, Barney shook Peter's hand and asked him, 'How do you make a garden like this?'

'Mulch and water,' Peter replied simply. 'And no digging—it stirs up the weeds.'

When I got home that day, I sat with Susan Irvine's book *Rosehips & Crabapples*, and found this diary entry:

Following the paperback edition of *The Garden at Forest Hall*, we get an increasing number of uninvited visitors. This is not always convenient but then I am reminded of the admonition found over the doorway of a Paris bookshop to '*be not inhospitable to strangers lest they be angels in disguise*'.

I felt that it was *us* collecting angels along the way.

Barney and I continued to visit a variety of Tasmanian gardens for inspiration, but none had quite the effect of Forest Hall or Wychwood. We returned home encouraged in our own ways—me to continue the tender loving care of the Nuns' House and Barney to turn his paddock across the road into a park. In March, my first birthday present to Barney was a red maple chosen from a local nursery. It was the first tree in the park-to-be and we planted it together, right in the middle of the paddock, so that I could see and appreciate Miss Maple, as we named her, from my front veranda.

It was more like we were seeping in love rather than falling, and I thought because of this it might last. Meeting a possible life partner in your forties is not like meeting them in your twenties, when love can sweep you off your feet like a tornado because you haven't lived that long, or at least long enough to ground you. You don't have to close your eyes and pretend that your destiny is marriage and mortgages either. You're not making the sort of calculations that people make about parenting abilities, social status or earning potential. You're not even having to please your own family or friends, because they gave up trying to influence your destiny a long time ago. I certainly had no intention of sharing the Nuns' House with a man, or of leaving it for one either. So, without a job title to our names, and undiverted by the instinct to procreate, we were free to meet each other, unadorned. Strictly speaking, as ourselves.

I was conscious that I didn't feel everything I was accustomed to feeling on rushing headlong into romance. There was no heightened expectation of the phone ringing (*is that him?*) or that appetite-suppressing gnawing in the bottom of your stomach that seemed to go hand in hand with new love. None of that *will I call, is he into me* shuffle that went on, or flirtation that kept you guessing. I wasn't looking for a knight in shining armour because I knew I could look after myself better than anyone else.

Those first four seasons together passed quickly, and although we couldn't recall the exact date we got together we celebrated anyway on the first of July with a bottle of bubbles by the river, promising each other another four seasons at least. Barn's scruffy paddock across the road was fast turning into that park he wanted, and the more I let down my defences, the more the Nuns' House lawns were mown. Annie teased she felt she was trespassing as she drove along Pipers River Road between us and that, despite their separation by road, our gardens were growing together in their beauty.

Richard Crabtree still dropped in for a cup of tea on his way to or from the vineyard. Audrey pottered out from time to time, holding up the traffic around the bends, she said, but I told her not to worry about that. Jillian sent Ian around to collect rosehips for her homemade foraged jams. 'Help yourself, there's plenty there,' I said. And every now and then Barn's dog found his way across the double white lines. I hoped that Harry wouldn't be run over while doing this because there'd be nothing fair in that. I could tell it was him by the sound of his nails clip-clipping on the polished floorboards, hurrying towards me, clamouring for a pat.

# Jilly's rosehip & hawthorn jelly

This is a late-season recipe using ingredients commonly found in hedgerows around fields in the Tasmanian countryside.

Equal quantities of rosehips (halved) and haws (the plump red berries of the hawthorn tree)
2 Granny Smith apples per kilo of berries, roughly chopped with peel and pips included.
1 tsp citric acid per kilo of fruit

Put all fruit in a large pan with just enough water to cover, bring to the boil then simmer for about 30 minutes, using a potato masher occasionally to release more juice from the haws.

When fruit has softened, transfer to a jelly bag, or double muslin cloth, taking care not to allow any fruit to escape.

Suspend this over a large, non-reactive bowl to drip through overnight or at least 6 hours.

Next, measure the amount of liquid you have and transfer to a jam pan.

Add sugar warmed in a low oven, cup for cup of liquid, and stir until sugar is dissolved.

Bring to the boil and boil vigorously until setting point is reached.

Bottle immediately into sterilised jars and cover while still hot.

The resulting jelly will be a beautiful ruby colour and the medicinal properties of both rosehips (very high in vitamin C) and haws (a renowned heart tonic) will guarantee you good health through the winter months.

# CHAPTER 14
## Spring, Karoola

Let no man say, and say it to your shame,
That all was beauty here until you came.

Couplet commonly found in parks around the world

Now that Wilf's garden was cleared, the light was making surprising things grow. A small oak tree seemed to have seeded itself (I recognised its distinctive leaf from Susan's garden) and a row of glossy green-leaved shrubs that I didn't recall being there last year had appeared at the top of the higgledy-piggledy dry-stone wall. Audrey had tried to remember the name and thought they began with A, so we went through one of the Stirling Macoboys and found them: *Acanthus mollis* or oyster plant. I never got the chance to find out what Wilf had in mind for the part of the garden he'd reserved, but at least it was less dishevelled now and, if he was anywhere, maybe he would make things grow the way he wanted them. Barney helped me to plant two boxes of daffodil bulbs we'd rescued from an old vineyard garden being demolished in Pipers River. And with Wilf's garden gnomes dotted underneath the trees I hoped he might feel more at home.

Aside from gardening, I visited Audrey for home-cooked suppers that usually involved sherry poured from a decanter and sipped from a certain glass. Ma, who would soon be eighty, was accustomed to living on her own and fending for herself, so meals tended to be on a tray for one. Every now and then, when she knew you might be visiting, she'd bring out one of her standards, a simple recipe cooked from her black-covered bible, *The Good Housekeeping Cookbook*, published in 1950. She'd taught herself to cook from it before she was married and now it was falling apart at the seams. 'Oh, this old thing,' she'd say, irritated at its stray pages that had come unstitched. But the precious black book still came out. I don't think Audrey ever approached cooking as a pleasure in itself. I imagined that as for many stay-at-home wives and mothers, it was more something she knew she had to do. I admired how she still made the effort to cook, although really, she couldn't be fussed.

I wasn't sure I would have got to know Audrey like this if I'd stayed in London. Whenever I visited from the UK we seemed to get under each other's skin. I think it was because I couldn't relax in her company, and I would return to London feeling guilty and relieved in equal measure. When you're consciously trying to parent yourself, a parent still parenting is suffocating. Whatever it was, we ironed it out and we had made it to friendship. I could sit with her in the middle of the day

watching *Ellen* on the TV turned up way too loud, her cigarette
smoke clouding the air, and not want to leave immediately. We'd
come a long way.

One day I came home from Audrey's to find a jar of fresh
blackberries on the front doorstep. It was a recycled jar, stuffed
with plump fruit, sat on a berry-patterned napkin in the middle
of the top step. There was no card but I knew it was a hello from
my friend Rose and the wilder boundaries of her garden. Nothing tricked up or fancy, just an expression of friendship in a jar.
I unscrewed the lid and popped the first berry into my mouth,
savouring it. The rest I'd save for an apple and blackberry tart,
already imagining the swirl of dark liquid as it seeped into the
apple amid dollops of thickened cream. I loved how, with a little
thought, someone else's surplus could become a precious gift.
And, just like the peace and beauty I aimed to preserve at the
Nuns' House, I never wanted to take the generosity of others for
granted, and returned Rose's offering with a tart.

The local tip opened on Sundays at 11 am but Malcolm usually
got there at ten so I headed off early with some garden rubbish not destined for the compost. Sure enough, there he was,
organising the old washing machines and sheets of corrugated
iron. He said he liked to arrive early so he could get things
'cleaned up' before the rush. For Malcolm, there was a place

for everything, and everything in its place: old farm equipment and water tanks, furniture and bicycles, a bin for cardboard boxes, another for vegetation, and a total of eight numbered skips. Rubbish disposal cost two dollars per trailer and it was one dollar per carload, until the council increased its pricing, much to the dismay of the locals.

A small hut sat just inside the tip entrance. At first sight, it looked like a lean-to, done up for a tip man to while away a chilly day undercover. A frayed armchair appeared welcoming in one corner, a bookcase with magazines lined the back wall, and there was a heater for cold winter days. Malcolm's self-styled retreat was actually a tip shop, and everything was for sale.

'How much for this old putter?' I asked.

'Two dollars.'

'The vase?'

'Two dollars.'

'What about this old oil can—isn't it sweet?'

'That'll be two dollars,' Malcolm said with a smile.

Libby arrived and, joining me in the fossicking, spotted some shapely wooden-handled leather-making tools. We chatted and agreed that sometimes the tip seemed more sociable than the village green: both rubbish and gossip got recycled here. I liked that there was a place for unwanted things to go where they might again be wanted, rescued from oblivion and restored by love and attention. With a little dust, a good wipe, a smear of O'Cedar and a place to live or a purpose, most things destined for the skip could be brought back to life. I noticed that things seemed to revive in direct response to the amount of attention received; that is, if you valued something, it would be valuable. This was different to putting a price on something. Things that had charm and were valued were priceless—valued in and of themselves. Because they meant something, they had worth. Because they were appreciated, they glowed. I thought this was something financial markets rarely understood and industry only ever regarded in extremes, either to plunder or ignore, like the tree farms that were now encroaching on Pipers River Road.

In four years, I'd witnessed much of the length of the road from the Nuns' House to the coast turn from pasture to plantation, and an improbably large pulp mill had been approved not far from here: up the valley a few kilometres, west across the Tippogoree Hills on the banks of the Tamar River. Many people in the local community had campaigned against it because of concerns about pollution. But that didn't stop the forest industry march, where uniform rows of non-native gums replaced native bush, scrub and farmland. Wildlife scattered, and so, too, did families who left for the city, the Western Australian mines, or the retirement belts of Queensland and elsewhere. I couldn't understand why *Tasmanian* native trees, like blackwood, myrtle and sassafras, weren't being farmed instead.

I understood the need for jobs, for paper from pulp and for timber for building, but when farmland changed so rapidly into plantations, and all you could see from the roadside, for kilometres, was one kind of tree, who would draw the line, and where? Who would say when enough was enough? I couldn't help but wonder if all the farmers in the valley decided to sell their land to forestry, and thousands of one species of tree were planted, how would it feel living here at the Nuns' House then?

Could lemon trees be tainted by spray? Would the groundwater be affected? How would I know? Would there be a chain of log trucks on Pipers River Road, and how safe would Audrey be driving the bends to see me then? When I had spent this time to craft a life, could it all be lost?

My dream to save Coronation Hall and turn it into the Pipers River Produce Hall, home base for a new food magazine and local market, was just that. Leigh and I had managed to save the hall from demolition . . . for just a few weeks, until the council caught up with its paperwork and the deed was done. Even though we'd convinced the local aldermen of the possibility of new uses, we had been unable to secure the funds to save it from the bulldozer. I guess I knew it would happen one day. But the day came sooner than I thought.

I was rostered to work at Jansz and took the shortcut to the vineyard as usual, turning into School Road and up the lane I had given avenue status because of how gloriously it was hedged, only to see that the hall had vanished completely. All that was left was a finely gravelled area where the building once stood. I pulled over onto the hard shoulder and sighed. There was no sign or plaque. Nothing to remind future generations of the times spent here at Coronation Hall, Pipers River. Its past was gone now, abolished by the council. And the private memories of birthdays, anniversaries, badminton tournaments, dances, celebrations and commemorations, of families coming together to share stories and the joys and tears and first kisses of their lives over seventy years, had been publicly erased, extinguished and then raked over carefully to delete any sign of their history. It was as if nothing at all had ever happened there; not even a shadow remained.

The disappearance of Coronation Hall made Barney and me even more determined to save what we could, when we could. One day, Barn had just finished his Lilydale school bus run; from the sunroom I saw him pulling into the driveway. He was excited because he'd spotted a massive pile of wood in the local sawmilling yard in Lilydale where he parked the school bus. There were some good-looking old timbers, sleepers, floorboards. The sawmill owner had said it was okay to take what we wanted from the burn pile.

'Come on, let's go,' said Barn, 'before it's too late.'

We both shared a passion to save, fix, mend, not spend. I only had time to grab gloves and hop in the ute next to Barn, while Harry was tied up on his lead in the back. The bonfire was the size of half a house. Hidden within it were sturdy old bridge timbers and massive beams that needed two to carry. We fossicked and lurked among the pile like wily old scavengers, selecting lengths we thought were salvageable. Barney tied down the ute load while I faffed around with ropes I could never remember how to knot. I was such a girl about this and, because Barn could always do it better and faster, it remained that way, although he often took time out to show me with no sign of irritation.

It wasn't hard to think what we could do with some of the wood. Ever since arriving here my books had been piled up in rows along the Nuns' House hall and corridor. Every time I tried to look for a particular book the Lego-like towers threatened to topple. I laughed when I saw photos of similar piles in posh interior design magazines, because people who have book towers could not possibly get to read them.

I had long held plans for a library. My brother Martin had suggested floating a bookshelf island from the ceiling. I liked the idea but it seemed too fancy for the Nuns' House. Les had done some research through his Tasmanian 'woodie friends': brilliant men who crafted wood with their hands. But the price was outside my budget. Meanwhile, bookshelves in second-hand shops seemed to be a dying breed.

Between us, it just sort of came together. We built the library from some of the timbers we'd salvaged, along with some old floorboards and bridge timbers that Barn had kept stored and dried underneath his house.

I chose as my library a nondescript spare room the nuns had once used as their chapel and we set to work, turning one whole wall from top to bottom into bookshelves. We worked well together, planing and sanding, sawing and bolting; sturdy floorboards were turned into shelves and handsome beams into uprights. It was hard work, measuring and fitting, without a plan, on a wonky wall, but after several days we finally stepped back and toasted the magnificent Nuns' House Library, made out of wood salvaged from a bridge. A home fit for books that had travelled around the world and back—twice. To reach the top shelves I found an old stepladder in a salvage yard which I spray-painted gold. Next, I dusted down the shelves and started unstacking the piles, revelling in finding a place for each book. Feminist texts went straight to the top shelf, while books about gardening, writers, photographers and Tasmania got prime space. While I sorted through them, some books spoke to me, seemed to have their own perfume, even enticed me to stop what I was doing and open them, only to find a name or year I could not remember writing inscribed on the title page, or revelations offered up from the past.

Wilf cherished his library, and after he died some of his books came to me. One, *Rubáiyát of Omar Khayyám*, had Wilf's signature scrawled on the inside along with the date, 1971. It was a volume he used to quote from throughout our childhood and it smelled of old bookshelves, dust and tobacco. I was hungry to find one verse in particular about a moving finger . . . I turned the pages one by one, scanned left to right . . . there they were, the verse and my father's words like Lazarus on the page:

> The Moving Finger writes; and, having writ,
> Moves on: nor all your Piety nor Wit
> Shall lure it back to cancel half a Line,
> Nor all your Tears wash out a Word of it.

Although he quoted it all the time, as children I don't think we really understood it, except we liked how it sounded profound. Hidden between two pages I found a piece of lined notepaper. It was stained with a coffee ring and scrawled in his doctor's handwriting: 'Democracy—A political system calculated to make the intelligent minority subject to the will of the stupid.' Ha, that was Wilf all over. Disdain for the ways of the world without the power, he thought, to influence it. I loved how his mind had touched the page of a book I could hold in my hands after he'd gone.

Our passion to repair and reuse found other outlets. On the hill behind the Nuns' House the outlook of the white weatherboard Sacred Heart Church was paramount. The church, completed in 1898, had a separate belltower and I'd always admired the big brass bell with its very own roof made of red corrugated iron—more agricultural than ecclesiastical. Even though services were held here every fortnight, I'd never heard the bell ring. In fact, the bell rope was missing. Between us we conspired to replace it. One evening, under cover of dark, we walked more briskly than usual up to the church. Barney pulled on his black 'ninja' gardening gloves and, while I kept watch below, climbed the tower like a monkey, attaching a length of rope to the old bell so that it could be rung out again across the valley. That night, we each took turns to ring the bell and decided we should walk up to the church every full moon to ring it out loud. Sadly, we learned that the church secretary had received a complaint from a neighbour about the bell pulling, so we stopped. However, a few weeks later our hearts lifted when we heard the bell being rung on Sunday morning for the 9 am service. Apparently it hadn't happened for years.

Every now and then, depending on how brave we were feeling, we'd stroll up to the church and give the bell rope a short tug. One evening, Dave Flynn followed us up the hill in his ute, we guessed on his council rounds. We stopped and chatted, and during the conversation he pointed to a massive gum tree and recalled playing in its tentacle-like branches as a child. Maybe it was the nostalgia in the air, the conversation, or the rogue in Barney, but he was the one who started it. We each took turns, pulled the rope and sounded the bell out over the neighbours' roofs, across the fields and down the valley. I think Dave might have smiled on the outside that day.

Some days it was harder to write than others. Interruptions stopped the flow or the concentration. Harry would visit, or Barn might drop in on his way somewhere for a hug or a catch-up. I would take a break to make three coffees in a row, but still no words would end up on the page. There were other distractions—like how to earn a living while I wrote. I wanted to remain creative and self-employed and not have to work full-time. So freelancing suited me, but I despaired a little when jobs were cancelled: three weeks' work at the radio, two days at cellar door, a commission to write a feature for an American magazine about a dairy on King Island . . . all cancelled for varying reasons outside of my control. I went for a stroll to see the garden still growing. *The planets may not be lining up for me*, I thought, *but they are aligned*. The silver birches were growing nearly a metre a season and my blueberry circle was slow but promising. The newly planted olive tree had definitely found its feet, the veranda's climbing rose had recovered because I'd learned how to prune it, while Les's echium seeds had taken and were now as tall and phallic as he had imagined them to be at the Nuns' House.

One day, Barn dropped in with a passenger he wanted me to meet. It was Billee, Dave Flynn's sister. He was giving her a lift into Lilydale to pick up her car that was being serviced. As a thank you Billee had made him two cakes. He favoured the cream sponge—all sweet, eggy and puffy—and I asked Billee if she'd mind sharing her recipe. She said she'd made it once a week for most of her life.

I later found Billee's recipe in the *Centenary Cookbook*, a collection of country recipes from the women of the Karoola-Lilydale Parish, compiled for the centenary of Karoola Sacred Heart Church (1898–1998) and kept in the State Reference Library. There was Mary East's Queen Mother's Cake, Heidi Robnik's Guinness Loaves and five recipes for sponge cakes alone, all with different combinations of eggs, cornflour, cream of tartar, bicarbonate of soda, warm milk, cold milk and butter. But Billee's? Billee's was the simplest and, I thought, the shortest recipe ever written. Pure essence of sponge!

Other interruptions were far less pleasurable and sometimes I struggled to make sense of the path life offered up, the turns in the road that shook trust and caused conflict. I especially wondered how this could happen while minding your own business at home. One sunny morning Barn had just returned from his morning school bus run and we were sitting having coffee on the Nuns' House veranda. We could hear the sound of a distant chainsaw; not uncommon in the bush, although it seemed closer than normal. Then there was a crash too awful to ignore, the sound of a tree falling . . . more chainsawing, and another crash that split and cracked. It sounded far too close for comfort, so we jumped in the car and went to investigate.

A council team was working in Waddles Road. The men had felled a line of the tallest trees and all that was left, like amputated elephants' feet, were their massive stumps. The Park Lane trees were gone, even the twin-trunk tree, felled in a chainsaw minute. We stopped the work by being there, which caused a confrontation, so we got straight on the phone to the council. It turned out that some of our neighbours had asked for the removal of several dead limbs overhanging the road. Instead of attending to just the dead branches, the council had negotiated with a local contractor who was prepared to clear-fell all of the trees for free, saving the council the cost of an arborist. If we hadn't stopped the work when we did, much of Waddles Road would be bare of tall trees for the most unnecessary of reasons.

I decided to drive into town to see Audrey for dinner. Barn didn't normally come but this time he did and it was the right thing to do. We felt taken under a wing by Mum and her Beef bourguignon with rice. We both voiced thoughts about leaving the corner, but instead reminded ourselves that, in all, we had managed to save eighteen trees along the roadside that would otherwise have been felled. From then on I changed my morning walk in the other direction—to Rowley Hill Road. Hopefully what happened that day wouldn't happen to others who cared enough about their roadsides to protect them.

I told Paul Broad the story of Waddles Road.

'Whatever happened to common sense?' he questioned. 'You don't cut down trees in the country because a branch might fall on you! You just have to be a bit more careful when you walk underneath them.'

*Sunrise on Rowley Hill Road.*

194

# Billee's sponge cake

4 eggs
1 cup sugar
1 cup self-raising flour
1 tsp vanilla

Whip eggs and sugar together with vanilla. Stir in
sifted flour. Bake for 25 minutes in a moderate oven
in two 8-inch greased and floured tins. Fill with
whipped cream sweetened with a tablespoon of
icing sugar.

# CHAPTER 15

## *Sixth summer, Tasmania*

Do not trouble yourself much to get new things,
whether clothes or friends . . . Sell your clothes and
keep your thoughts.

**Henry David Thoreau**

I don't know why people think it's quiet in the country—there are always so many jobs to keep you occupied. Every day I felt useful, and at the same time helpless because there was so much to learn, so much that I could do better, or at least get round to. I reminded myself not to be ruled by the jobs or by perfection. If people visited they would have to ignore the dusty floors, the dirty windows, cobwebs, unweeded beds or unfinished jobs. I would get round to them, eventually.

Shearing was one of those things in life I could not do on my own and I always approached the task with a degree of dread. Although I didn't want to rely on Barn, he offered to help corral the alpaca ready for the shearer, and arrived one morning with a very long rope. As we strung it out across one corner of the paddock, Barn showed how just a gentle flick of the wrist on the rope was enough to hold the alpaca where they were. We tied off each end to make a corral around the pump shed which had a power outlet so Ian could shear on the spot. I didn't know if Stuart and Rosemary were watching from the top of the hill, but if they were they would have noticed the difference that a few years had made. In their rope corral, Jack sat down—he knew what was about to happen—while Kerouac pushed his nose into the air in defiance. At this point, neither made any attempt to escape.

When the shearer arrived, this time, Jack and Kerouac were ready. 'I remember him, he's the screamer,' said Ian. 'We'll get to him first.' And he was right. Kerouac loathed being shorn, and I still found his screams unsettling, but the sight of Ian's Shih Tzu puppy sniffing around prone alpaca hooves relieved the tension. It was a shiver of a dog, but Ian's lifeline, he said, as his wife had passed away not so long ago. Jack, meanwhile, grinned and tolerated the indignity in silence and seemed to be soothed by Ian speaking softly in a language that sounded like a cross between Finnish and Icelandic (lots of improbable consonants). Vaccinations were done, then teeth and nails trimmed, and the job completed in under half an hour or thereabouts. They looked so different without their fleece, and seemed to not even recognise each other. I paid Ian and we gathered up the wool on the ground, filling another four large garbage bags to hang on the shed wall. Another job done for the year.

With the alpaca groomed, it was my turn. These days I dressed in grunge. When I worked at British *Elle* magazine in the early nineties, 'grunge', made fashionable by Nirvana, was defined as wearing the first thing you reached for in the morning—clothes by the bedside, left over a chair, the first top in the drawer that felt right rather than what you thought might look right for someone else. I dressed without thinking, which meant I mastered the art of wearing flannelette pyjama bottoms that worked in bed as well as in the garden: warm, roomy and uncreasable. And in summer, it was sawn-off jeans and long-sleeved shirts to protect my arms from the sun. Jackets no longer seemed to have a purpose unless they were for warmth or waterproofing and wouldn't look out of place in a paddock.

Early autumn was in the air and I spent the morning in the garden collecting baskets of twigs from around the wattle and gum trees ready for the first evening fire. I remember Elma, one of Audrey's friends, had called them 'morning sticks'. She was in her nineties and told me how collecting twigs and branches used to be one of the children's jobs when she was growing up on a farm in Longford; her particular chore had been to polish the lamps and keep them filled with oil.

Barney decided to open up a hobby nursery and had propagated some plants and picked up others from trips to nurseries near and far. I helped him move the old chicken coop and loved how he transformed it into a potting shed, complete with a stained-glass window. A shade house was added, followed by two long polytunnels. He laid old house bricks in different shapes under the shade of trees, and plants and trees were lined up on them in orderly rows. There was running postman, grevillea, callistemon, silver birch, lavender, Japanese maples, blackwood trees, populous and pin oak, stone pine, dawn redwood, shelves of pretty miniature cyclamen, ferns and box hedge, and conifers of all description. What sold was what survived in his hobby nursery, in natural conditions, and nurtured with the utmost care. One or several of each variety were planted in the paddock, then mulched, manured and watered in a methodical way, so that visitors to the nursery could see how their garden might grow.

We came to know the corner where we lived as 'Karoola Corner'. The hard bend that opened up onto a mile-long straight was a joy for drivers. Barney could tell the sound of a Ducati even before he saw it, and often we'd stop to watch a motorbike or car of particular note slow for the bend, and then accelerate. I liked living on the road, but the corner was not the safest place to stop and nursery sales relying on passing trade proved slow. The signs would go up at nine in the morning and come in again at six. Sometimes, for many days in a row, no one stopped. I could tell Barney was despondent but he kept watering, potting and repotting, and the plants and trees at Karoola Hobby Nursery looked stronger every day.

Like me, he wanted to be able to make a living where he lived, not commute to offices that wasted time and took you away from where you wanted to be. We reminded each other this was a virtue that we hoped would bring about good things; it might just take time. 'It is what it is,' I would say. 'It is what it is,' echoed Barn.

When the Lilydale market first opened the following spring, Barney decided to take along his plants to sell. If there hadn't been a town crisis, the market may never have happened. When plans became known for a new forestry plantation to be established on the edge of the town, through the sale of private farmland to forest investors, it was a bridge too far for many residents who felt the tranquillity and safety of the village would be threatened. Signs were posted around the district, and many community meetings were held in the memorial hall. Logging families filled the back rows and others turned up just wanting to have their say or to hear more about plans that concerned them. A village green meeting was held in Lilydale. There were speeches and songs but some workers at the sawmill behind the green chose to fire up their chainsaws in an attempt to drown out proceedings. They even made it onto the TV news.

In the end, the sale to forest enterprises for plantation purposes didn't happen. Instead, the land was purchased privately and the battle lines stood down. But for some a bitter aftertaste remained. The community met and opted for mediation to come up with positive ways of coming together. One of the suggestions that came out of these sessions was to hold a fortnightly village market.

Barney and I were keen to support the market and adapted his ute with removable shelves for the purposes of carrying as many plants as possible. The nursery was Barney's, and although I was happy to join him I was keen not to blur the lines or step on his territory. So I decided to do my own thing with seeds and herbs. I collected a few seeds from the garden and sorted them into small brown paper bags, which I stamped with a gold butterfly and labelled as 'The Nuns' House Seeds'.

There were sunflowers, Italian parsley, calendula, love-in-a-mist and my favourite, old-fashioned fragrant sweet peas that I'd first bought in a small packet from an elderly couple at the annual Longford Flower Show. I potted up a few herbs and, early on market morning, cut, tied and labelled bunches of fresh herbs from the garden and put them in mini tin buckets. Les had given me a black moleskin book to write in, and I opened it up for the first time to record Barney's and my first trip to market. Inside, on the first page, I wrote:

Sage
Mustard Cress
Basil
Sweet Pea (seeds)
Coriander
Italian Parsley
Love a Sunflower (seeds & potted)

We set off early for the first Lilydale Village Sunday Market when the day was still cool. It was hard work loading all the plants into the ute, and just as hard taking them all out again at the market. Barn arranged his plants in a sweeping semicircle and his retail brain made him conscious of things like traffic flow and space for prams, concepts I hadn't really considered. At the end of the day we counted up our takings and I made a note in the little black book:

Herbs/Seeds $65
Plants: $400

The stallholders agreed that the market had been a great success but the lack of fresh produce needed to be addressed. After all, how could you have a market without produce?

'Why don't you sell produce, Hil?' pressed Libby, who was there selling homemade preserves and her mountain spring-water. 'Instead of your produce hall, you could bring it to market. I know a farmer you can buy some veg from. I'll have a word with him, get you together, and you can go from there. What do you reckon?'

Two weeks later, in time for the next market, we sourced potatoes, onions, pumpkin, rhubarb and carrots from a farmer in Scottsdale. We gathered apples and apricots from orchards in the Tamar Valley and strawberries from the pick-your-own farm at Hillwood, and had harvested spinach and lettuce from our own gardens. Inspired by French village markets, we used wicker baskets and second-hand basketware for the produce. Together we cut up small boards and painted them with blackboard paint to chalk on our prices. We bought a gazebo to keep the sun off the produce, and made a rustic table out of recycled fence palings to place and arrange baskets of cherries, berries and apricots. Any money we made from fruit and veg went into a tin and became our fund for sparkling wine.

With plants as well as produce the stall looked abundant and full of life. You could tell that Barn had run a fruit and veg stall before, and I loved the way he reached for a peach or a tomato when customers stopped to browse: 'Here,' he'd say, 'try this.'

'Would that be a Moorpark apricot?' asked one customer.

'Oh, I don't know exactly,' I replied. Stupidly, I believed an apricot was an apricot. In fact, I couldn't remember ever seeing the specific variety mentioned on labels in the supermarket. I vowed to have the answer next time and to know the difference. There was always so much to do in preparation that the need to know *what* I was doing was preceded by the actual doing of it. Of course, that was no excuse.

With a cup of tea in hand on the Nuns' House veranda later that day I found the space occurred for idle thoughts, where there were no distractions, when *doing* slipped back to *being*, and the time was spare to have a different slant on the day. So I thought about the slightly imperious woman with a wide-brimmed hat who stood and asked me to serve her two kilos of potatoes in a bag.

'I'm selling vegetables now,' I remarked to Barney over a meal that night. 'That lady. That was the moment I realised— I'm selling vegetables!' In my head, I felt good about reaching this point on this day, doing these things, with this man who said he loved me as well as *us*. But all that the customer in front of me could see was a woman with potato dirt under her fingernails selling fruit and veg. I felt discomfited by her expression—she seemed to look down her nose at me—and yet I had no compulsion to explain what I had done in my life before this moment. Just like the wardrobe of jackets still sitting in plastic bags in my bedroom, destined for the op shop, that path might have brought me here, but no longer mattered. What mattered was that the stall looked wonderful, we sold out of produce, took $180 for fruit, veg and herbs, and $390 in plants. Between the two of us, after costs, we made $175 on the day—which, naturally, we spent on bubbles. 'What I'm doing,' I thought, 'is who I am.'

None of this was planned. It happened organically. When we got to share the day like this, what we did with our time was our way of life and that was precious. It wasn't about having your own desk, knowing your place, playing a role, leading a team, paying off bills, saving up for holidays or tying down a relationship. It wasn't any of this. It was a philosophy lived rather than discussed and dissected and we felt no need to rush. The Nuns' House had taught me to sit back, see what presented itself, and leave space for the future to happen. Preparing for the market was exhausting work, though, and I wondered how farmers could find the time to take their produce to market when they were so busy growing it. It took two of us a day to get it together, to pack and prepare; to weigh then bunch rhubarb with rubber bands or carrots with thick string; to polish apples; to weigh and arrange strawberries lovingly into punnets (start with four large ones in each corner then fill up the centre with smaller fruit) . . . Up early to pick delicate herbs before setting off to market and when you arrived home it still wasn't over—there was always more to do. But a sense of fulfilment nuzzled up to the dusty exhaustion we both felt at the end of each market day.

The blueberry season had started and one blue-sky Sunday I headed off to Crestview orchard in Lebrina, not far from Lilydale. I now ranked picking blueberries at Crestview, alongside a swim at Lulworth Beach, as one of the highlights of my north-eastern summer. Crestview's paddock looked almost as full of vehicles as a Woolworths car park. And there was so much fruit that each branch looked weighed down like a giant eyebrow touching the ground. This was something families did together and it was hard not to listen in to their conversations across the blueberry hedgerows. Nothing really important was said—just the little irks and joys of life shared along with a love of blueberries. Some picked in one place leaning over the bushes; others sat on their haunches and picked their way up through the branches. Whichever, buckets were soon filled to the brim, and children ran back to get more. The loveliest thing was realising not every blueberry needed to be picked, and how you could only see this in times of abundance. It felt good to be able to leave the not-so-ripe for someone else to pluck. The truly blue, silver-coated plump berries nearly bursting at the seam were the ones to prize, ready for eating, not keeping. I packed eight kilos, picked in ninety minutes; 7.5 made it home . . .

Throughout summer we continued to go to market every fortnight. We sourced produce from other growers, too, and got to know the locals, who came to support us. Many older people liked to stop and chat and asked about where things came from and how things were grown. Like Clair and Bob, a retired couple from Underwood. She would hand-select their fruit and veg for the week, while he trailed behind her with a carry bag and a wicked sense of humour. Suzanne from Lalla liked to look for particular plants for certain spots in her garden. I remembered her as 'the lovage lady', because one Sunday she came especially with her husband to give us a small pot of lovage they'd dug up from their garden. I only knew the name of it from a play I'd once seen in London's West End, *Lettice and Lovage* starring Maggie Smith. It felt connected now that I had the actual plant in my garden and could appreciate its strong taste and elegant lime leaves.

I decided we needed a practical shopper bag for customers, along with our biodegradable plastic bags. After much futile research online, we decided to make them, sourcing hessian potato sacks from the local rural supplier. Cut in half, each sack made two carrier bags. Barn had a roll of upholsterer's hessian that made excellent handles, and the final touch was a machine-stitched label made out of stiff brown paper. I used an ink pen to hand-write the inscription. I tried the words 'Fruit & Veg' but decided 'The Nuns' House' had more warmth.

My friend Vivienne had come to visit from Italy on her self-styled 'grey gap year'. This was the year she retired, sold her flat in London and was travelling to see friends around the world before settling in . . .? She knew not where. She would make that decision when the time came. Originally from the Shetland Islands, it was no accident that she had fallen in love with Tasmania. Pity they were as far apart as they could be.

Viv spoke fluent Italian and was the kind of retiree who wore bikinis, scarlet polish on her toenails and went bungee-jumping off bridges. She had freedom because she had chosen it and that meant she could be here, now, adding this masterful touch, sewing up the top edge of our market bag in big woolly blanket stitches. Both of us remembered learning blanket stitch in our childhood, probably in the Brownies, and it took a few goes to remember that the stitch went backwards. We sat on the back veranda bathed in February sunshine, sipping wine and making bags together ready to take to market. Viv stuffed one with newspaper and modelled it while I took photos. We stitched and sewed into the evening and Viv decided a puttanesca supper was the way to go. She explained puttanesca came from the word *puttana*, which is Italian for prostitute, and roughly translated means 'prostitute style': being so quick and easy to assemble they allegedly used to make it between clients. It was pure Mediterranean sunshine. As she spooned it into the bowl, Viv said it never looked like enough but, cooked properly and with a handful of parmesan tossed over it, it was richer than you thought. And she was right.

On market day, we priced the bags at six dollars and hung them from the gazebo roof. When a young woman bought one I watched with pride as she hooked the hessian handles over her shoulder and strolled casually around the market with our handiwork on show.

Simon, an accredited green plumber and renewable energy design consultant, ran the market with his partner Carmencita. She came from Sicily, had a PhD in Asian Studies and taught tango dancing. Together they baked wood-fired pizzas on market day, and there was always a queue at their stall. Gina was there from Yondover Dairy in Tunnel with her artisan goats' cheeses; she hoped to open a cheese-tasting room on her farm next year. Tanya sold organic blueberries and raspberries harvested from Honeywood, the Strongs' family farm in North Lilydale, and Libby Macbeth, a medical herbalist, was lining up her homemade pots of native flora ointments and creams. Jillian and Ian sold Jilly's homemade preserves, and brought their alpaca to show. The Honeychurchs from Pipers River sold golden pots of leatherwood and bush honey, and Stella, who was Argentinian, had baked fresh ciabatta. We encouraged Crabtree to come along with his wine, which he did, and it was a great success, if only because the stallholders could have a glass of his pinot noir or chardonnay while going about their business.

Barn liked to take a break and wander off, but always returned with pizza or fresh cheese and we'd sit in the shade of the ute and think about how lucky we were to have such riches on our doorstep. We were amazed by the variety of stallholders within our neighbourhood—hardworking, multicultural and creative. It was a colourful site on a Sunday and the village came to life. Both sides of the road were lined with vehicles and all the businesses seemed to benefit from the extra visitors the market attracted. The usual politics applied when people were required to rub along together: there was tough competition for stall sites and the staking out of territory was fierce. The next-door stall quibbled over the space we were taking up and by next market we noticed the lines on the ground were painted a little more sharply. One stallholder played country music far too loudly, and there was a united plea to change the tune and turn it down.

One day in April, the market was cancelled due to heavy rain, which left us wondering what to do with kilos of fresh potatoes, carrots, onions, rhubarb, pumpkin, parsnips, plus capsicum, cherry tomatoes, sweetcorn, silverbeet, apples and spring onions. We wanted to try to cover the cost of produce and decided our best option was to box it up and take it to town. While the rain pelted down on Sunday afternoon, we set off to Jansz to collect recycled Vintage cartons, and made up six boxes to look as fresh and overflowing as possible. We did this by feel. What would *we* like to see in a box of fresh fruit and veg? We took a photograph of the contents of one arranged in a basket, sitting on Barn's back veranda next to a bottle of our local sauvignon blanc. If you didn't know the view overlooking the Pipers River valley it could almost be Tuscany. After emailing family and friends with the image and a message, we managed to sell all six boxes and covered our costs within a day. We were happy not to have wasted good produce, and happy too that people seemed impressed by the freshness.

In late May the market closed for winter so we decided to continue with our 'rainy day business model' for fresh produce boxes. We wanted produce to be as 'just-picked' and local as it could be, which meant we collected it on the weekend ourselves direct from farmers, packed it on Sunday night, and delivered on Monday morning. Above all, we wanted our venture to pay for itself. We decided to call ourselves 'hilbarn'. When an academic friend asked if we'd chosen it as a take on 'Barnhill'— 'You know,' he said, 'the remote house in west Scotland where

George Orwell wrote his novel *1984*'—we had to confess that no, we weren't that clever. We chose it because it was a combination of our names.

Within a couple of months, we'd more than doubled our customers, to fourteen box subscribers, and could no longer fit the boxes into the car. On the way home from one of our delivery runs we spotted an old Ford Transit van for sale in a pub car park and decided to take it for a test run. It was a 1978 model and reminded me of the van in *The Italian Job*.

'What do you think?' asked Barn.

'I'm happy, as long as it goes up hills.'

Barn dipped into his cash reserves until the business could pay him back, and that was how we came to own our first fresh-produce delivery van.

By the end of the year we had forty box subscribers. We began a blog because it seemed the easiest way to tell the story of the produce we bought and where it came from. Together we had accidentally become hunters and gatherers of fresh local produce packed in a box. I yearned to celebrate what was grown in our region and to share our passion with others. And I loved that others seemed to want to do the same, because our business was growing fast through word of mouth.

Barney used his corporate background as an oil company pricing analyst to build a spreadsheet, recording all the data the business needed, from customer information and future payments to egg orders and suppliers' contacts—a complete financial system for hilbarn. I preferred to write things down, freehand, in the black book. I also loved to find new growers and saw it as a journalistic task. Between us we seemed to be able to cover most things. Each week we asked each other if we had ten more customers could we still do it? We both agreed to continue as long as we were having fun. Instead of a produce hall or magazine, I felt pride in having found a new market for growers, and that it had blossomed accidentally out of our own imaginations as a way of spending time together.

We converted the Nuns' House tool shed into a packing shed and bought a second-hand coolroom to help keep the produce fresh. Our neighbour Rhonda came to help us pack. We'd sourced our own boxes by then and the three of us worked through the seasons filling them up on Sundays for Barn and me to deliver on the following morning. We chatted about how a lettuce should be packed, in plastic or newspaper, whether tomatoes should be loose or in brown paper bags, if apples should have their stickers on, and how different herbs might be bunched. All the things we did we learned along the way. Barn would say, 'It's about how it feels.' And I'd think back to the *Cosmo* days in London and the mad hours, sometimes *days*, spent around a table with Marcelle, Vanessa, Tania, Kath and Bev, conjuring snappy lines that would fit on the cover. 'Is it grabby enough?' 'We need Flakes!' '. . . and gingernuts!' 'Send the workie!' In those days, Marcelle would light up an Alpine to have with her strong tea and the coverlines were eventually born, typeset and tweaked again before finally being committed to press. That's how great magazines were made then, nothing to do with marketing science or focus groups, everything to do with *feel*.

The skill in making up a fresh produce box was about the love expressed in putting it together so that nothing was automatic. It started with a few apples, then a bag of potatoes, freshly dug, tipped into a brown paper bag with the corners twisted into ears, then a large swede or a handful of carrots with their bottoms all poking up, and a bunch of ruby-coloured rhubarb lying diagonally across the top . . . There was a point (no one was ever quite sure when that was) when one of us stopped what we were doing, stood back and said, 'Wow, great box this week!'

Every Thursday, Des from the Lilydale School Farm came to work with Barn to make up our hilbarn boxes. His job was to stamp and tape the custom-made cardboard boxes, line them with fresh newspaper, and stack them ready for labelling. These were important but repetitive tasks and he did them well, although sometimes at a slow pace, without complaint. Des had very few words and too often the weight of the world seemed heavy on his teenage shoulders, while his trousers dragged on the ground. Other days his stories were joined up and full of life, about his relatives on Flinders Island, the budgie show he was saving up to go to in Hobart, or his fishing days with his uncle. One day I watched mesmerised while big Des chopped firewood in my driveway with the strength and grace of a ballet dancer and I told him that.

# Vivienne's puttanesca sauce

extra virgin olive oil
1 onion, finely chopped
2 cloves garlic, finely chopped
4 anchovy fillets, chopped
1 small red chilli, deseeded and finely chopped
2 tsp capers, rinsed and drained
small tin pitted black olives, quartered
1 tin diced tomatoes
½ tsp sea salt
¼ tsp freshly ground black pepper
pasta of your choice
1 tbsp chopped flat-leaf parsley

Heat the oil in a frying pan over a medium heat and cook the onion for 5 minutes, stirring occasionally.

Add the garlic and anchovies and cook until the anchovies meld in. Add the chilli, capers, olives, tomatoes, salt and pepper, and simmer, uncovered, for 10 minutes, stirring occasionally.

While the sauce is simmering, cook the pasta. Drain the cooked pasta into a colander and put the sauce in the bottom of the serving dish. Top with the hot pasta and toss together gently to combine.

Decorate with chopped parsley.

Serves 4.

# CHAPTER 16

*Spring, Tasmania*

It was spring again and the apple blossom was budding pink in the Nuns' House garden and in orchards from Hillwood to Spreyton as we trekked across the countryside in search of the first broad beans of the season.

'Give it a couple of weeks,' we were told in Spreyton. 'It's still a little early.'

We'd been sourcing produce and packing boxes every week for two years. Every week except Easter and Christmas. We thought we might have to limit the number when we reached a hundred boxes a week, but when that happened and we were still getting new inquiries for our boxes, it didn't feel right to turn around and say no. We expanded to take up the whole of the Nuns' House three-bay shed (the hay bales were moved out), and bought a second, postbox-red delivery van we called Versace (he was a bit flash in a 1985 kind of way). We moved into our second coolroom having outgrown our first, and ordered a third pallet of one thousand cartons. Paul and Jeff were helping us with van deliveries, and Bron, a raspberry grower from nearby Underwood, joined us to help pack on Sunday nights. We'd been written up in national newspapers and magazines and we owed all of this, having never paid for advertising, to word of mouth.

Weighing and bagging 120 one-kilo bags of potatoes is a repetitive task but not a monotonous one when it's what you want to do. The task is as heavy or as light as your mood. We reminded ourselves that there were downsides to every job and this was better than office politics any day. Above all, it was real. Rhonda kept us entertained with the ups and downs of farm life: new calves, fighting roosters, and the fattest free-range eggs we'd ever seen. Bron brought homemade biscuits and cakes for us to try and, when she returned from holidays in Europe, arrived with a bottle of apple schnapps, four tiny glasses and a photo album of her eating cakes across Europe. 'Hil, they're *real* cakes,' she said, already missing them, 'not like ones you get here.'

Those were the ups. The downs were never the bottomless downs I used to feel in London, the black moods I now associated with living in my mind, detached from nature. It was hard to feel good about the coolroom freezing over, though. I opened it one morning to find the temperature reading minus 1.9 degrees. We'd practically queued for the very first apples of the new season, now they were covered in a halo of frost. Five hundred zucchini, freshly picked for us the day before by hardworking Lebrina growers Michael and Liz, were as hard as a baseball bat. Six boxes of mushrooms and 550 nectarines that Barn and Des had picked from Barney's orchard the day before were unsalvageable. It was Saturday, the day before packing, and we'd have to start sourcing produce from scratch. We found our up, though, when we contacted all our growers again and they helped us replace what we'd lost without drama.

For months I'd been on the hunt for a local asparagus grower. On a fresh delivery morning, Barn and I had just finished our run in Launceston when I spotted a shop sign on the pavement that read 'Fresh local asparagus'.

'Stop the van!' I yelled.

Barn stopped at the next traffic light and I sprinted across the road, through the traffic, into the deli and straight up to the sales assistant.

'Fresh asparagus, finally! Where's it from?'

'From Victoria,' she said, shamelessly.

'Well, that's not exactly from-here local,' I replied. 'Thanks anyway.' And as much as I loved asparagus, I left the store empty-handed.

That's how much the bug had got me. I was so committed to the hunt for local asparagus that if it wasn't Tasmanian I'd rather not have asparagus at all. So what if Victoria grew ninety per cent of the country's harvest—why weren't we growing our own? I'd heard that it was difficult to grow, that it took some years to establish a crop, that it was tricky . . . nothing, though, that relieved my sense of frustration. I even accosted visitors at Jansz's cellar door who liked to stop and chat. One woman, a market gardener from the north-west, gave me hope. She said she'd planted an asparagus patch that cropped beautifully by the second year. Unfortunately, she wasn't growing enough for our boxes, but she wished me luck.

Such unplanned conversations spurred me on in my hunt for local asparagus. As a last resort, mixed with the foolishness of hope, I googled the words 'Pipers River' and 'asparagus'. To my astonishment, up popped 'Pipers River Asparagus'. It looked like there was someone growing it in my own backyard. I tracked down the number and rang the farm. 'Well,' said a woman's voice, 'we *were* growing asparagus but you're a bit late—we stopped last year.'

It was deflating to have come this far only to be just a few months too late. Judith proceeded to tell me why, despite growing asparagus for many years, they had given up. For one thing, it was backbreaking work as the spears were cut by hand at or just below the soil surface. Another, she explained, was the way of the supermarkets. The point of asparagus was to eat it as fresh as possible before the natural sugars started turning to starch, undermining both the flavour and sweetness. But the supermarkets, Judith said, wouldn't allow them to deliver their harvest directly themselves. They had to wait for a truck to collect and transport it to a central depot where it might sit for days, before being transported back to the supermarket. This so affected the quality of their crop that they had given up in despair. It just wasn't worth it anymore.

I wanted it to be viable, and while on the phone did my best to try to change her mind, but their decision had been made. In my dreams I craved, somehow, to help make growing asparagus worthwhile again, if not for Judith, then for someone else. I was starting to get a sense that growing produce might be an endangered occupation, because growers didn't seem to receive the respect deserved for the work they put in. I remembered the ad I'd seen in the old newspaper archive and thought, *I want to pay the most for cream.*

All around the Tasmanian countryside were homes with old dairies, cattle yards, chicken coops, barns and farm sheds, many of them derelict and no longer fit for any purpose. It was obvious that self-sufficiency used to be a rural way of life here not that long ago. But it was no longer the way of life; old barns seemed more sought after as backdrops for wedding shoots or as storage for toys, gadgets and tools that had fallen out of fashion. In the letting go of this way of life, I thought, maybe we had let go of running our own lives?

Each weekend, we travelled far and wide to collect freshly harvested produce for our hilbarn boxes. As much as we were passionate about supporting local growers and buying fresh, I wasn't sure we would do this every weekend if we didn't enjoy the road trip. I never tired of the journeys Barney and I took, whether together or alone. There was always a market or roadside stall that invited you to stop and fossick, or people who sold flowers from their garden arranged in colourful bouquets. We stopped the van and turned it around when a mass of red and pink proteas caught our eye for five dollars a bunch, 'includes plastic bucket'. One of our hilbarn followers wrote on our blog that our trips 'gave new meaning to market research'. Then, there were the views of natural landscapes that took our breath away.

On one of these journeys, while browsing in a roadside fruit and veg store, I finally spotted what I'd been looking for all these months: generous bunches of green asparagus in old plastic buckets. They looked local, sort of roughish, not perfect or conformist like the identikit spears found in supermarkets. Instead, some were fatter than others and they looked just-cut, showing healthy white bottoms rather than the cardboard grey signs of starch and age. I asked the counter assistant for the name of the grower, and she happily gave it to me.

'That's Jo. She doesn't have a lot but give her a call, she's not far from here.'

We rang Jo, who said that it was only a small patch and that she hadn't been picking a lot because of her back. Her husband had promised to make her a special picking chair, but he hadn't got round to it yet. If we called closer to the day of picking next week she'd have a better idea how much she would have. I must have sounded utterly desperate when I offered to help her pick.

'Boy, you're keen, aren't you?' said Jo.

'Well, yes, we really want fresh local asparagus that is fresh and local!'

'Okay, look, I'll do what I can.'

Barney rode his motorbike to collect the asparagus from Jo in Sassafras, roughly ninety minutes from Karoola. Thirty kilos fitted perfectly into two bike panniers and he arrived home with flushed cheeks. The roads were no more than lanes in places, winding through timeless countryside where red dirt and bright green produce-filled paddocks fronted blue Bass Strait—like agriculture-on-the-sea.

That night we sat at the kitchen table weighing and tying asparagus bunches with pieces of jute string. They looked a million dollars, as fresh and cared for as they could be. Hopefully people would appreciate the effort Jo had made—and hopefully she wouldn't break her back when we asked her to do it all over again next week.

Once the bunches were done, we put one aside for us, nine spears tossed into a shallow pan of softly boiling water, for just two or three minutes, long enough to make the spears gasp and wilt ever so slightly when you picked them up. We sat at the kitchen table and ate them unadulterated with our fingers. These were good days—long, but good.

I loved the way Barn and I cooked together and seemed to finish each other's dishes like other couples finished each other's sentences. Even though we lived opposite one another, we ate together most nights. We each had baskets that crossed the road filled with food (sometimes cooked and still bubbling), pans, bowls or glasses that got left behind last time, and bottles of wine. Recipes lived on as well as memories, like pears poached in green ginger wine, a reflection of our nights together.

Karoola Corner wouldn't be the same if Mount Arthur didn't dominate our view. It's one of Tasmania's higher peaks, home to the mystical burrowing crayfish listed as a vulnerable species, and the remains of temperate rainforest that had long been logged. We often found ourselves jumping into the car to chase a lightning storm round the mountain, or driving to the snowline to touch the snow. We loved taking the road partway to the summit, to stop at the forest river that passed under the road and walk to the top, or thereabouts, to take in views across Bass Strait. We named one section Fern Corner and took photos of each other waist high in lush serrated ferns that seemed primeval. I loved the quiet beauty of the roadside, how nothing had been planted, how it seemed to have always been there, and how what looked like scrub from a distance was actually, close up, an exploding galaxy of plants.

# Mountains are the beginning and end of all natural scenery.

John Ruskin

One Friday, we were stunned to see Fern Corner had been logged for woodchips. The route to the top of our ancient mountain, blessed by native bush and wildlife, had been scraped clean of all vegetation, destroyed for at least a generation while it self-healed. Mountain lovers who craved summit roads would first have to trek through a version of Armageddon, made worse because it was industrial. Why, we wondered, were public routes of immense beauty, and which gave access to local wilderness, still being treated with such a lack of care or regard by those entrusted to look after our forests? Without warning, seeing the devastation in this place our hearts might so easily be moved to melancholy or despair—and for what? Woodchips sold offshore for hardly any profit now.

Barney's teenaged kids were with their dad for the school holidays and I liked to invite them across the road for supper, raiding the recipe books and loading the table with comfort food. A big platter of meatballs in tomato sauce was their favourite, or corned silverside with parsley sauce and mash. The family of four arrived together, bearing baskets filled with wine and offerings for the table, and hugs at the door, one by one. I liked the table set and laid properly, which Billy loved to do himself, always finishing it off with a vase of flowers he'd picked from the garden. Rachael would bake a cake while James could eat twice as much as Barn. Although I wanted a simple life, I'd never thought of myself as old-fashioned, yet sometimes I felt I was with Barn's kids around. I only knew the rules that I'd grown up with, not the rules of today. I didn't know their music and thought every song sounded like Britney Spears, but apparently there was a whole other generation after her. Then the family—the father with his children—would leave to go home across the road and the Nuns' House returned to the quietness of being one. I loved and regretted the way this happened—it left a gap between us—and wondered what it was like for them, as kids, shuffling back and forth between their parents. I thought of all the different ways that families came together, though, and decided that maybe, seen in that light, it wasn't as bad as it might have been for them.

To help Dave out on the farm, and to give her something of her own to do, Lyndy decided to start breeding hens and selling free-range eggs and chickens. We started offering organic eggs to our hilbarn customers and I enjoyed hopping in the Jeep on Sunday afternoons and driving up the road to collect the eggs. There was always something new in the farmyard Lyndy wanted to show us: a hen that was so broody she'd taken to sitting on an apple; or a beautiful silkie who'd just hatched nine chicks and was playing mother hen. One day I arrived and the hens and roosters had arranged themselves artfully in Dave's barn on the back of his ute, as if they were waiting to be painted. We took photos and Lyndy shared her farmyard stories on our blog in the hope that our customers would see their eggs came from real chickens cared for by real people who told funny stories. I watched as Lyndy hand-polished the last egg to fill the dozen and was sure that her care could be tasted in the yolk itself.

This week our order from Alan in Northdown was our biggest to date: silverbeet, pak choy and basil. We first made contact with Alan after spotting his bagged fresh herbs hanging on the wall in a veggie shop only to find that he was a third-generation broadacre farmer who supplied the major supermarket chains. The herbs were something he enjoyed doing and was aiming to expand. He was more than happy to supply us with whatever we wanted.

The first time we met, Alan had given us a tour of his latest on-farm ventures—there were new polytunnels for growing hydroponic vegetables and a hothouse for micro herbs. His super-sized hands marked him out as a farmer through and through, but there was an air of mad professor about Alan as he played with new ideas and invented ways of making them work. Satisfying the supermarket duopoly was becoming increasingly difficult, he told us, with their compliance regulations now several pages long, including specifications for the exact sizes and dimensions of a cucumber. To us, a cucumber was a cucumber—all that mattered was that it tasted good. We wondered which came first: the customer who wanted the perfect shape or the corporate buyer who demanded it?

Alan's farm was organised with farm-made signage; capital letters were handpainted in white on green-painted wooden boards. There was OFFICE, HANDWASH, GRANARY and VISITORS REPORT TO RECEPTION. For customers who collected fresh produce from his big coolroom Alan made smaller signs out of brown-laminated, hexagonally carved board, carefully handpainting the name in gold letters.

We placated Ruby and Midge, the farm guard dogs, and opened up the coolroom to find a whole pallet of boxes just for us. Sitting on top was a wooden sign with the word HILBARN inscribed in gold paint, and a slot that held our invoice. For some reason the sign meant so much to us we both had tears in our eyes. Alan wouldn't have made a sign and painted our name on it if he didn't think we were here to stay.

Alan turned up. 'I'll have beans next week if you want them,' he said. 'You'll have to come and pick them for yourself though.' Alan explained that although it had been a good season for beans and the harvest would be a large one, the processing company wouldn't take the entire crop they had contracted him to grow. Instead, what they didn't take next weekend he'd be digging back in.

'What a waste!' we chorused.

We decided to pick beans for our boxes and arrived again at Alan's early on Sunday morning. Barn dropped me off and continued west to pick up brussels sprouts from Nathalie and Johan in Kindred. As Alan drove me in his ute to the bean paddock, his two dogs ran alongside, faster than the ute. The dirt was orange-red, the beans bright green, and the sky like a double shot of blue. I wasn't expecting Alan to stay, but he got down on his knees with me and together we picked the tiniest scratch of his broadacre paddock clean of dwarf green beans. He even showed me how best to do it by hand: first, kneel, don't bend. Pull out the plant, roots and all, turn it upside down and shake it so you can see the beans hanging in the opposite direction to the way they grow, then strip the beans individually by tugging down on them. Toss the stripped plant into a pile and the beans into a box. Aim to pick nine kilos in one hour between two people—that's talking while you do it of course, and allowing time to watch the dogs playing in the paddock and a break for a can of soft drink.

I loved being outdoors talking with Alan, but it was hard,

manual work, and perhaps not the sort I was minded to do every day. I looked down at my hands and nails that were cracked and split, tossed away the memories of manicures in London spas and held onto the thought that at least we had green beans.

Autumn was a breath of fresh air away. Barn and I collected produce along lanes lined with hawthorn trees starting to turn bright red with berries. It was also the last day of blueberry picking at Crestview. It was sad to say goodbye. I felt a sense of gratitude, loss, and yearning for more, all rolled up in one. But we'd be back next year. Happy 1 March, happy birthday Barney, wearing gumboots, getting caught in showers on cool nights, with open fires, stacking wood, pruning trees, kicking leaves, sipping hot chocolate, eating apple and rhubarb crumble together with dollops of thickened cream . . . *I love the seasons we share.*

Oddly, March was also the month in Tasmania when the forest industry decided to start forestry burns, when the sun could be extinguished at midday, and highways closed by poor visibility caused by nuclear-sized mushrooming plumes of smoke. Despite calls from asthma sufferers, from concerned residents, from schools whose students couldn't get to school, from winemakers worried about smoke-taint on their grapes, the industry continued with its practices. No one could understand how this could be allowed to happen in a place that also sold itself on being 'clean and green'.

As the seasons turned I felt less and less inclined to visit cities, but it was definitely my turn to visit Leigh in Sydney. When I arrived at the departure lounge at Launceston airport, I was stopped by a security officer who asked me to take off my shoes, belt and jacket. As a Londoner, I used to be able to justify the discomfort of undressing in public in a busy airport with the thought that at least our security was being considered. But who in their right mind would make Tasmania a terrorist target? Why, I wondered, did we want to be like everyone else, or to play by their rules, when we were so obviously set apart?

A second officer stopped me and explained politely that her job was to swab for traces of explosives. Would I stand aside please and hold out my arms? I surrendered in despondency to an invasion of privacy in a place where I had hoped privacy meant something. After living in Europe and travelling all over the world for nearly twenty years, I'd never been so thoroughly searched prior to boarding a plane. It made me want to stay home.

I remembered when the first American bombs were dropped on Baghdad in 2003. I was working at *Closer* magazine on Shaftesbury Avenue. I remembered how we gathered around the television to watch the bombing and I thought to myself we were watching an act of murder. How these acts still touched my life now, years on, in the swabbing of my body at a small domestic airport—so exquisitely provincial you still had to board the plane via portable staircases pushed by airport ground staff across the tarmac and pick up your luggage from a tractor trailer—was incomprehensible to me. I got to Sydney, drank cocktails in a brand-new bar in the Cross, bought a pair of gold wedge-heeled boots, swam laps in the Boy Charlton pool, ate breakfast out, and talked with Leigh almost non-stop for two days. That was my Sydney. It fed me, and although I'd lived there for four or five years, it wasn't home; at least, not the kind of home with constancy at its heart.

You must know that feeling of arriving home: the ease, the sense of comfort when you open the door, put down your bags and breathe in a familiar air. I had found this at the Nuns' House. And now I was finding it with Barney too. He was waiting in the driveway with two glasses of bubbles when I got home. How simple are life's true pleasures. Accounting for his height, he lifted me up and stood me on the back step so I didn't have to crane my neck back to kiss him. Then I threw open all the doors and windows and said hello to every view: the view from the kitchen window of rolling hills and a country road, and paddocks crisscrossed with fences and stocked with cattle and sheep. Through the sunroom window I could see the wiggly line of willows running along the creek, Karoola corner, and Barn's paddock hurrying slowly into the park of his dreams. From the front veranda, the soft humps of the valley hills were kissed by afternoon sun, and in the foreground the lemon-tree smile was beaming. A car passed and pipped. We couldn't see who it was but we each threw up a wave anyway.

Isis, one of hilbarn's customers, had left a recipe on the hilbarn blog using the Lebrina beetroot we packed into last week's box. I always tried to photograph the produce we collected in natural sunlight on rough backgrounds, just as they were. I always took a few options. Usually it was the first one that worked because it was how I had initially seen it, without trying to make it look good, to consciously find the right angle, arrange the leaves, make the light stretch, lose the shadows, or paint a perfect picture. First-feel was what seemed to work, even though sometimes it was out of focus.

Isis's recipe for beetroot chocolate cake sounded so

incongruous I had to try it. Morning light shone straight into the Nuns' House kitchen, making it one of the most pleasant times of the day to cook. The boiled beetroot was blitzed into a puree and poured into a chocolate cake mix. The sunlit colours of purple and chocolate looked ravishing as they mixed together, like paints in a bowl. I poured the beetroot-chocolate mix into an old heart-shaped baking tin, one of our market finds, and took photos with my phone at the same time. The cake rose more than I thought it could, which made the top crack into two magnificent ravines. It tasted as it looked: perfectly confounding. We shared the recipe online with thanks to Isis and her love of Liz and Michael's Lebrina beetroot.

## Isis's beetroot chocolate cake

'I ♥ beetroot!!! Here is a lovely chocolate beetroot cake I made from the last beets I got from you.'

*Isis St Pierre*

75 g cocoa powder
180 g plain flour
1 tsp baking powder
250 g caster sugar
250 g cooked beetroot
3 large free-range organic eggs
200 ml vegetable oil of choice
1 tsp vanilla extract
icing sugar to dust

Preheat oven to 180°C and lightly butter a 20 cm round cake tin.

Sift the cocoa, flour and baking powder in a bowl. Mix in the sugar.

Blend the cooked beetroot in a food processor. Add the eggs, one at a time, then the oil and vanilla.

Process until smooth.

Make a well in the centre of the dry ingredients, add the wet mixture and lightly mix.

Pour into cake tin and bake for 50–60 minutes or until a skewer inserted in the centre comes out clean. Cover loosely with foil if the cake starts to brown at 30 minutes (expect the top to crack!).

Leave for 15 minutes before removing from the tin, then place on a wire rack to cool.

Dust with icing sugar to serve.

# CHAPTER 17

## Spring, Tasmania

I once sat opposite an elderly man on the train from New York to Boston. We shared the sort of open conversation that people do when travelling with strangers they are never likely to see again. 'I could never tire of that view,' I said to my new train friend, as I looked out of the window at the Manhattan skyline. 'You remind me of my late wife,' he beamed. 'Every morning of our married life she would wake up, wish me good morning, and say, "What shall we do with the day?"'

That's what the dawn birdsong inspires in me followed by the welcome light of the sun as it breaks over Mount Arthur. The urge is always strong to open a window or a door into the early morning, no matter what the temperature, to smell the dew, the perfume of a new day with the promise of things to be done. Today, the blackberries seemed to have ripened suddenly. I could tell because Jack and Kerouac were raiding the fence for breakfast. I grabbed a billycan and headed down to the bottom paddock to see what was left. *One for me, one for the billycan, one for me . . .* Barn stopped on his way home from driving the school bus and helped to pick and eat a few. We left just enough in the bottom of the billy to make an apple and blackberry tart: apples from our gardens, blackberries from the paddock fence. I loved these roadside suppers and that a fence could be edible too.

The next time I collected eggs from Lyndy she had some news. She and Dave had got engaged and were wasting no time in naming a date. It was going to be a country wedding held in their backyard with family and friends, and Barn and I were invited. She was over the moon, but, being more accustomed to living in comfortable farm clothes, she had one concern: the dress. I told her I could see her all bosom and hips in a dress like the one Marilyn Monroe wore in *The Seven Year Itch* with the white pleated skirt that blew up around her legs.

On the day of their wedding, Barn and I laughed out loud at a huge handpainted banner tied to their cattle yard that read 'Farmer Has Found a Wife'. So many friends and family had gathered to celebrate the occasion that Dave and Lyndy's front paddock was full of utes and cars. We parked, and as we walked up the farmhouse driveway towards the back garden I spotted Lyndy in a sky-blue strapless dress, its silky skirt floating and billowing like summer clouds. Wedding guests were chatting in the shade of the shed where Dave's vehicles were normally parked. Trestle tables were laid out with an abundance of plates, platters and bowls carrying their friends' home-cooked offerings of cakes, meats, fruits and salads. Rob from the Lily-dale service station was sparking up the barbecue, dressed uncharacteristically formally in a shirt and tie. As we made our way to the garden that was full of scented rosebushes I stopped to admire Lyndy's handiwork. She'd made a large sun umbrella out of stiff cream calico, pegged it over the Hills hoist washing line, and tied it on with big blousy bows. Seats from the Karoola Hall were arranged underneath the now shady clothesline in a semicircle. We all sifted in, gradually, and found a spot ready to hear the celebrant's words and the couple's exchange of vows.

Lyndy and Dave, both in their fifties, a lifelong spinster and bachelor, looked as happy as the frolicking Suffolk sheep in their paddock and the free-range hens nesting in their honeysuckle and rose bushes. I hadn't known either of them for very long, but I felt thrilled that they'd found each other late in life and wanted to share the rest of their lives together.

Barn and I continued our Sunday road trips from Wilmot in the west to Winnaleah in the east, and Lefroy in the north to Tea Tree in the south, picking up produce as fresh as it could possibly be. The Shingle Shed near Latrobe was an old fruit and vegetable shop with dim lighting and a concrete floor. We usually dropped in on our travels to have a look at what was there, and to browse through the nursery next door. On one of these occasions, Barn spotted two trays of perfect lettuces—red and green mignonettes, misspelt as 'minuet'—and as pretty as a bouquet. We asked the woman behind the counter if she knew the grower.

'No, but if you like I'll call the owner to find out.' She popped out the back to use the phone and soon returned.

'Sorry, she can't remember his name. Thinks he's somewhere

up Port Sorell way. She doesn't have a contact. The man just drops in with his lettuces every now and then.'

'Look, we'll take all of them,' said Barney. And we left the shed smiling with two trays of perky lettuces. They were grown hydroponically, so when it came to packing them, Rhonda wrapped their wet spidery roots in newspaper and we sat them on top of the box like a gift.

I was haunted by the perfect lettuce and felt compelled to track down the grower so that we could buy more. Alan lived near Port Sorell—perhaps he might know?

'I think he might be somewhere near Thirlstane,' said Alan. 'I probably shouldn't be telling you this—he could be competition!'

I decided to drive to Thirlstane—it was only just over an hour away—to see if I could find the lettuce grower for myself. I stopped outside houses, drove up driveways, knocked on doors, and stopped one woman tending to her horses in a paddock— but to no avail. I turned back onto the main highway and was heading for home, feeling thwarted, when I noticed a ute pulling into a driveway.

I stopped to ask the driver if he knew a man who grew lettuces in Thirlstane.

'Yeah,' he said, 'he's right over there.' And he gestured over my shoulder to the house next door. There in the garden next to a greenhouse was a man tending to trays of lettuces.

'Thank you,' I said to the man in the ute. 'You've made my day.'

We'd never noticed the hothouses before, even though we'd driven past them nearly every weekend. Funny how sometimes you never really see what's in front of you, even when you know what you're looking for.

The man was attending to what looked like twenty rows of a thousand lettuces growing at waist height in small channels. It was bitterly cold, with alpine winds coming straight off the Great Western Tiers.

'They're living lettuces—it's hydroponics,' explained Graeme. 'I'm still learning.'

He told me that he worked as a nurse at the local general hospital but started growing lettuces a few months ago because he wanted to be closer to home to help his wife Kym look after their two young daughters. 'I'd love to help you out with lettuces,' he said, picking out two for us to try.

I often wondered how it was that Barn and I had grown up in different ways and places and yet our feelings for things could be so in tune. We both liked finding and rethinking unwanted things, and to love and preserve what was local. An old farm gate cast aside in a paddock could make us turn off the road. We always checked with the farmer first and offered him something for it: 'It's our heritage,' said Barn. I learned that on rainy days farmers used to keep themselves busy by making gates. Certain wooden styles with crosses were my favourite—you rarely saw new ones like that. In the end, we made one together out of recycled wood for Jack and Kerouac's paddock.

On the way to picking up fresh produce in Scottsdale, we used to say hello to an old Ford truck that had been left in a paddock to rust. It was a 1975 Ford D Series, with a long timber tray and a racing-green cabin. It had a look about it, and when Barn said it had good lines, I knew exactly what he meant. One

*Gate at Northdown, Thomas Estate, overlooking Bass Strait.*

day we dropped in to the farmhouse next door and introduced ourselves to the owner.

'We'll make you an offer if we can get it going,' said Barn.

The next day, we set off with tools in the boot and my bucket containing pink rubber gloves, a dustpan brush, Jif and cloths. Audrey would have been proud of me. 'I don't think we'll worry too much about cleaning it until we know we can get it going,' Barn said.

'Yes,' I said, 'but I'd like to clear out the cobwebs and grease before I sit in it!'

After fitting a new battery, Barn put the key in the ignition and turned it over without the accelerator to get the oil into the engine. After pumping the accelerator a few times, we both cheered when the engine started straightaway. Michael Brill, the owner, couldn't remember how long it had been sitting in his paddock; he thought at least five years, maybe more. 'She used to carry logs, was as tough as they came,' he said. Barn soon worked out that a metal brake line had broken which we'd need to fix before moving her out of the paddock. I left Barn and Michael working on the old girl together and set off to get brake fluid from the nearest service station twenty minutes away.

The next day we went back to the truck and Barn fitted the new brake line. We did a lap of the paddock and decided she was good to go. There was no one at the house so I left some cash in an envelope under the front door, and opened the gate to let Barn out onto the road. I followed in the Jeep thinking, *the things we do together.*

A few weeks later, and on her second attempt, the old Ford truck passed her registration. Barn texted Michael with the exciting news and he replied: 'Well done! I trust she will serve you as she did me, got big heart. Brilly.'

'What are we going to do with a truck?' I asked Barn.

'I don't know, but we saved it,' he said with a smile and a hug.

The first feature I ever wrote for British *Vogue* was about collectors. One smart man collected all sorts of jugs—but only white ones—and displayed them in tall, purpose-built glass cabinets in his drawing room. Another, a twenty-something woman who lived in a downstairs flat in South Kensington, had a collection of pig ornaments. When I asked her how it started she told me 'with one pig'. After that, people started giving them to her as gifts and, before she knew it, she had a collection and had been collecting pigs ever since. I realised this was how we came by Maurice, an old Morris Commercial J-type baker's van. If I hadn't told my friend Leonie at Jansz about how we'd rescued a truck from a paddock, we would never have known about the sweet van that her husband had bought for sixty dollars in the 1970s and that was now rusting away in their back shed in Pipers River.

'You can have it,' she said. 'We don't want anything for it. It'll be going to a good home.'

According to the midday news it was the day after the world was supposed to end. Lyndy had emailed to say that between them the girls had only managed two dozen eggs this week. Petal, she wrote, had decided to go broody, and had been sent straight to the broody box, but Blanche had started laying and was producing a good-sized egg: 'People don't realise the stress behind producing a dozen eggs!' she wrote, and signed off saying she and Dave had been blessed with another set of twin lambs: 'Luckily the world didn't end after all . . .' We let our customers know that their egg order would have to go on hold as the chooks were on vacation; like everyone, they needed a rest now and then.

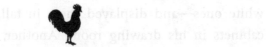

I was keen to track down some old photos of the Nuns' House and thought of Dave Flynn's sister Billee, the kind lady who'd given Barn the thank you cakes. She said she wasn't sure what she had but would have a look. I should give her a couple of days to put her hands on them. Then, just before hanging up the phone, Billee told me a friend of hers used to live here as a nun.

'Yes, at the house where you are. She lives in Launceston now. She's no longer a nun, though. If you like I'll give her a call and let her know what you're after. She might be able to help you.'

I was excited at the prospect of meeting someone who could connect me to how the house used to be.

A couple of days later Barney dropped in to see Billee and she handed him a manila folder, a photo album and a large envelope to give to me. They felt like treasure in my hands: newspaper cuttings, stories of the old pioneers and of the building of the church on the hill. Two black-and-white photographs

*Karoola congregation photographed at the opening of the Sacred Heart Church, November 1898.*

*Opening day of the Sacred Heart Church, Karoola, in April 1902.*
*(Photographs courtesy of Billee Parry)*

of a massive congregation featured tough ground and smart country people dressed in their finest suits and frocks, with an array of bowler hats, bonnets and boaters, fashionably de rigueur for early settlers in 1898, photographed at the opening of their church. She told me the collection had come to her from her grandmother, who had organised the church's fiftieth anniversary. The community's history was alive and looked after in Billee's care.

There was also a copy of an article from *The Monitor*, dated 4 April 1902, on the opening of the new convent and a welcome to the Presentation Sisters—quite a showy name for nuns, I thought:

They will indeed have the warmest of welcomes from those dwellers in the Turner's Marsh and Karoola districts, who have kept alive under Tasmanian skies the best Catholic traditions of the old land, and who have infused into the hearts of their children a love for their Holy faith, that rivals in its intense devotion and its practical character the faith of Holy Ireland itself. The old pioneers are passing away—the men and women who so bravely faced the perils and the hardships common to all the early settlers—but their spirit of faith and their example of pluck and plodding perseverance remain, and in the happier times now before them will bear simple fruit.

I liked those words, and the ideas that sprang from them, of aspirations to bear simple fruit, of folk full of pluck and perseverance. There was no mention of the convent here at the Nuns' House, and no photos, but, as promised, Billee had also included a handwritten note with the name and phone number of her friend Louise Lee-Archer, the nun who once lived in my house. By phone, Louise had a warm and lively voice and was more than happy to share her memories of her time in Karoola. She had some photos she'd hunt down, she said, but she'd also given a lot to the Catholic library and suggested I contact Sister Carmel in Hobart. I invited Louise to visit the Nuns' House for morning tea the following week and I was thrilled when she agreed.

It was a chilly enough morning to light the fire, although the skies were clear and the borrowed scenery outside my window was picture perfect, as if the valley had put on its Sunday best for Louise's visit. When she parked her car at the front gate and hopped out, I was pleased to see she was as lively as her voice.

'Oh, that view from the top of the hills as the valley opens out,' she sighed. 'I'm surprised no one has captured that in a photograph to promote the district. It truly is a beautiful valley. You know, I think of it as my valley?'

'So do I,' I said, standing on the front steps. 'Welcome back.'

I noticed how Louise took special care not to step on the brass footstep at the front door. 'It used to be my job to clean and polish it!' she recalled. 'I was always in the habit of stepping over it because of that—so I'm not going to step on it now!'

And we both laughed at her memories. She placed her bag and a book on a chair, and I let her take in the surroundings while I made us both a cup of tea with a plate of Nuns' House shortbread.

'There used to be a corridor here,' she said, tentatively. 'That was my room—well, it's where I slept. And there used to be a sink right there.'

I loved listening to her spirited memories of the house: how she watched the football played on Karoola oval from the front veranda; how the dining table was always piled high with church correspondence; how the elderly Sister Finn Barr slept in the little room off the front veranda, the one I used as a study, and that Louise, then Sister Claver, would never dream of entering. She told me how the nuns used to catch the school bus to Lilydale from the end of the driveway.

'The school bus was really a lorry with canvas sides,' she laughed. 'The prefect used to say to the children, "Siddown or I'll knock you down!" We'd get in wearing our long black habits and starched white guimpe. It was a gravel road from Karoola to Lilydale so by the time we got to school each day we were filthy!'

She remembered ringing the bell up at the church to tell the farmers to stop their milking and come to mass, as well as setting the rat-traps behind the altar.

'I dreaded taking them out—it would make my stomach turn but I would tell myself I was doing it for the Lord.'

I would never understand the strength of her belief, only that she must have loved her God more than life itself.

She peered inside the pantry and recalled how it had always been full of preserves. 'It looks like they're the same shelves . . . We'd give the bottles back to the people of the parish and the ladies would fill them up again with fruits. We always had good food because we had to be healthy to teach, and being in Karoola we always had the best vegetables.'

Louise took her vows as a Presentation Sister at the age of sixteen. She knew that she would never go back home unless one of her parents died. It was a simple life, living in cloisters, where they shared everything. The nuns worked hard but were never paid and consequently never had a penny.

The book Louise had arrived with turned out to be a hand-written journal complete with photographs. As soon as she mentioned it, as much as I wanted to delve inside its pages, I didn't want to ask. Inside she'd recorded her eighteen years of life as a nun, as well as her later years as a single woman, teacher, wife and mother. I would need more time to take it all in and hoped she would feel comfortable enough to leave it. Louise found one photo—a loose one—taken in the front yard of the Nuns' House. Then she turned to the pages on Karoola. There she was, as Sister Claver, standing with her family on the old school steps of the Nuns' House.

*Louise Lee-Archer (Sister Claver) with her family (left) and with*
*schoolchildren (right) at the Nuns' House in the early 1960s.*
*(Photographs courtesy of Louise Lee-Archer)*

Louise told me that she loved her four years in the valley, and that the people of Karoola had given her a feeling of worth. She said she liked country places—'perhaps because they represented the freedom I didn't realise I was longing for at the time'.

We chatted until lunchtime, when Louise had to leave. I waved her off from the front steps. As she drove out, I noticed that instead of turning right back to Pipers River Road, she turned left up to the church to take in the view of our valley.

*The Archbishop of Tasmania opening the new Karoola convent in 1953;*
*this is now the Nuns' House veranda. (Photograph by K. Malcolm,*
*The Standard, p. 1; courtesy Wallis Centre Archive scrapbook,*
*Archdiocese of Hobart)*

*Children dressed for first communion on the Nuns' House front steps.*
*(Photograph courtesy Billee Parry)*

# Nuns' House shortbread

250 g butter, softened
⅓ cup caster sugar
1 tbsp water
2 cups plain flour
½ cup rice flour
2 tbsp white sugar

Preheat oven to 160°C. Place baking paper on two oven trays.

Beat butter and caster sugar until light and fluffy; stir in the water and sifted flours in two batches.

Knead on floured surface until smooth. Divide dough in half; shape each, on separate trays, into roughly 20 cm rounds. Mark each round into 12 wedges; prick with fork. Pinch edges of rounds with fingers; sprinkle with white sugar.

Bake for about 25 minutes; leave on tray for 5 minutes. While still warm, cut shortbread into wedges along marked lines. Allow to cool.

# CHAPTER 18

## *Christmas, Karoola*

I can scarcely wait til tomorrow
when a new life begins for me,
as it does each day,
as it does each day.
'The Round', Stanley Kunitz

The rain is running off the tin roof, funnelling and gurgling down the gutter at the side of the study as it makes its way to the old underground concrete water tank that I hope will last the torture of another summer without cracking and leaking. The arched backs of Jack and Kerouac are just visible as they graze in their paddock of long grass and white daisies under the glow of a double rainbow.

Mild anxiety is brewing like the distant thunder: we have a hundred orders for Christmas berry boxes, all paid for, but we still don't know if there will be any fruit. With so much rain, the strawberries have had no time to ripen, and we've heard the cherries are splitting due to the constant downpours. The blueberries will come when they come and not before. No one can talk, bribe, seduce, nag, harangue, negotiate or turn them into being. It's nobody's fault, but it means that the last few days before Christmas will be a runaround to see who has blueberries, if the raspberries are ready, and if enough strawberries can be picked to fulfil every order. And cherries? I need to call Frank and Nancy.

Nearly forty years ago, Frank and Nancy planted roughly seventy cherry trees on a pretty hillside in Underwood at the end of Cherry Farm Road. One of my favourite views in springtime is of a sun-drenched lane that meanders through their orchard, down to the old chalky-blue wooden cherry shed. The dog scampers ahead, ready to take on the moment in the midst of all that blossom-madness. How incredible it was, I thought, that in roughly eight weeks' time all those pretty flowers will be plump and luscious cherries. Last year we watched with amazement as the dog picked cherries off the tree and ate them.

'Hello, Frank, how are the cherries?'

'What cherries? We'll be lucky to find a single one!'

'What, not one kilo?'

'No, not one cherry! It's the worst season we've ever seen. They're all splitting. Call again at the end of the week but we can't guarantee anything . . .'

As much as we'd like to buy Frank and Nancy's cherries we decide it's best to look elsewhere.

In the country, the daily weather forecast seems just as important as the daily news, and rather than being a trivial way to pass the time a chat about the weather comes from a deep care for mutual livelihoods. Farmers know their fortunes are dependent on the season being kind to them and that their egos can never be bigger than the seasons.

'Rain . . .' they say. 'Drought . . . Ya cop it on the chin.'

I envy people like Frank and Nancy who have seen their trees through nearly forty summers: the knowledge they glean from that is not the sort to be found in a book. Sometimes I think it's only in the *practice* of growing and caring for something that has particular needs—in that ground, on this hill, with that aspect, through those years—that you learn what needs to be done. Travelling might give you a different perspective on where you are, but in settling you reap the reward of each season by turning with it. In this way I think I've come to understand that who I am is where I am.

I now have the satisfaction of knowing certain things about the Nun's House: that the veggie patch grows best in a raised bed on a flat terrace at the back of the house, for both sun and water; that if I stop mowing the west-side paddock in early winter it will be blanketed hot pink with ixia bulbs in springtime; that the eastern paddock yields between forty and sixty bales of hay, depending on the season; that if I don't cut back the dead spikes of the October-flowering watsonias they will look statuesque later in winter on a frosty day; that if I plant in early autumn the ground will still be warm enough for growth, but if I plant later, in spring, the growth will be slower. In some ways, living by the seasons is like watching children grow: you have something to measure the years.

Ever since moving to Karoola I'd considered keeping chickens. I know friends in city suburbs with pocket-sized gardens who have hens so it's natural to have them here, although not natural to me. There's a suitable pen in the backyard that Rose said could be adapted, but I've worried about them being caged up or not being here to look after them so settled on reading about them instead. Somehow, though, seeing Lyndy's chickens scurrying about in her garden rubbed off and I've decided to get two. I settle on two striking buff-coloured ladies, one slightly blonder than the other, with sexy legs and underskirts all petticoated and frothy, and name them Marilyn and Monroe. While picking them out, I noticed that Lyndy had recycled her wedding marquee into an extra chicken coop. 'Needs must,' she said. 'It's better used than getting mouldy in the shed.'

From the advice I'd read and received I decided to keep the girls locked up for two weeks to get them accustomed to their new home. I hated seeing them running backwards and forwards along one side of the fence as if demented, so when the two weeks were finally up I opted to leave the gate to their coop open.

Each night they found their own way back to the nest

and let themselves out of a morning. This seemed to go on like clockwork. I watched as, together, they started strolling up the gently sloping hill to their den, pecking a grasshopper here, an ant there . . . At a certain time of evening when the light lowered, they knew to enter through the open gate and put themselves to bed. When the day shortened, so did theirs. I tried to clock them each day to see if their bedtime matched the hour the sun left the day, but my own life wasn't that ruled by time precisely so I gave up.

My hens taught me things I didn't know. I learned that they cluck loudly after laying an egg, and will find you if they're hungry. They won't eat what they don't like and will always leave a little grain in the plate for later. If you lay down mulch in the garden they will find it straightaway and scratch it out of place. Regardless of your efforts to put it back they will remove it again each time as if they think they're helping you, when in fact it's quite the opposite. They clean themselves by flapping their wings and rolling in dry dirt baths they make by digging in the garden, sometimes so well they look as if they'd buried themselves. Now they've made a nest in the honeysuckle bush where they lay perfect buff-coloured eggs. I love going to the nest when the eggs have just been laid and are still warm to touch. It feels like stealing but I always say thank you to the ladies as I carry them inside. Nothing quite like hour-old eggs, poached in a pan of gently rolling water for three minutes, then laid on toasted homemade buttered ciabatta. When the planets are lined up I get two eggs a day; some days, bizarrely, there are three . . .

This is as far as my smallholding goes. In another six

years and seven summers, maybe I will have mastered limoncello, crop rotation, a sunflower paddock, and spinning alpaca
fleece . . . Of course, I'm only just scratching the surface. I look
at Suzanne and Alvaro's vegetable garden in Lalla—their raised
beds, the intricate planting, savvy ways with irrigation, the rare
varieties of vegetables and herbs, some saved for seeds, the neat
footpaths lined with sawdust, and the immaculate quality of
everything that is in season, trussed, tied or pruned, mulched
and composted exactly as it should be—and feel overwhelmed.

'I have so much to learn,' I said, standing in the middle of
it all.

'But I didn't start until the age of forty-five,' said Suzanne,
with all the encouragement in the world. 'You need to get a
copy of *Guide to Vegetables and Fruits*, from the Rodale Press.
It's how the organic movement started. Look it up.'

'A lot of people would like to live this life but put it off,'
said Alvaro.

We stopped to listen to the squeaky-door call of a family
of native hens. To Alvaro they sound like a cross between a
donkey's bray and a rusty saw. 'I consider it a privilege to hear
a native hen,' he says. 'It gladdens my heart when I hear them.'

Suzanne and Alvaro came to Tasmania from Chile in their
forties. Thirty years on, they still think of themselves as 'city
people' but their vegetable garden is a masterpiece of the life
they now lead. In Chile, Alvaro had worked as a naval architect,
senior executive and lecturer, holding five university degrees,
but in Tasmania he chose subsistence farming. Suzanne said one
of her favourite things to cook from the garden was Tongue of
Fire, a strikingly beautiful green bean tipped with red flames

which hails from South America. 'It's a special family occasion for us, as the beans must be harvested at optimum plumpness, but before they start to dry.

'In Chile, I remember seeing sacks of beans with their edges turned down: white beans, pink, striped, beans with spots . . . I used to dream of making a mosaic out of all those beans. In South American popular culture, beans give strength and courage. We've been planting ours and saving the seed for thirty years.'

'You must select pods with the maximum number of beans,' said Alvaro. 'From those, eliminate the smaller beans. The bigger ones have more energy.'

'Come back when the beans are ready,' said Suzanne. 'Come and eat with us and I will make *granados con choclo*—it's a traditional summer dish from Chile.'

Back at the hilbarn packing shed, Barn had made a hundred hilbarn berry boxes out of recycled fence palings with the help of Des, Anthony, Nathan and Michael from the Lilydale School Farm. They look heavenly lined with gold florist's paper and wispy 'wood wool' shavings, waiting to bear fruit and take off. We had traversed the berry triangle from Turners Beach to Underwood and Ross, and finally sourced the best fresh berries we could find. The coolroom looks like Christmas.

With Rachael, James and Billy home with their father for Christmas we all pack together, and finish off the berry boxes with sprigs of holly picked from the roadside by Barn and his eldest son, James. We add up all our costs and at the end of all the calls and visits to growers, the making, weighing and packing and the delivering, we have a grand total of thirty dollars,

which makes ten dollars each for the kids. That's how it works;
it is a Christmas harvest, after all.

As promised, we received Suzanne and Alvaro's invitation
to join them for beans picked from their garden and turned into
'simple people's food'. Barn was busy doing gardening work in
Lalla, so Suzanne said we'd save him some leftovers. The beans
were served straight from an earthenware pot onto a flat plate
with sliced tomatoes from the garden, drizzled with a little oil,
garden basil and freshly cut chilli.

'How do you say *bon appetit* in Chile?' I asked.

'Ah, this is *buen provecho*,' explained Alvaro. 'In Spanish,
this means enjoy your meal, but *provecho*, literally, means profit.'

*Buen provecho!* When you eat from the land, you profit. If
only we could all learn how to look after the land like Suzanne
and Alvaro, I thought.

# Suzanne's *granados con choclo*
## (fresh leather-pod beans with corn)

1 kg fresh beans, shelled
250 g pumpkin, diced
1 onion, chopped
2 cloves garlic, chopped
1 tbsp olive oil
paprika and fresh chilli, chopped, to taste
fresh oregano, chopped
½ red and ½ green capsicum, diced
250 g zucchini, diced (optional)
kernels from 2 corn cobs
salt
basil, handful of fresh leaves
5 ripe tomatoes

Wash the beans, cover with water and bring to
the boil. This water may be discarded if you wish
(to minimise flatulent effect); in this case, bring a
fresh pot of water to the boil, add the beans and
the pumpkin, and simmer gently; the fresh beans

will cook rapidly, so don't overcook. Do not add salt until they are tender.

In another saucepan, sauté chopped onion and a little garlic in some olive oil, add some paprika and a bit of chilli and oregano.

Add capsicum (red and green), perhaps some zucchini, then sweat, covered, for a few minutes before adding these veggies to the beans and pumpkin. Add corn (sliced raw off the cob). Season with salt and add some of the basil.

Simmer gently for flavours to mingle; the consistency should be saucy but not soupy.

Serve with sliced ripe tomatoes drizzled with olive oil and sprinkled with basil, and offer fresh chopped chilli if available.

Serves 5 to 6.

# EPILOGUE

*The Seventh Summer*

If the day and the night are such that you greet them
with joy and life emits a fragrance like flowers and
sweet-scented herbs, is more elastic, more starry,
more immortal—that is your success. All nature is your
congratulation, and you have cause momentarily to
bless yourself.

**Henry David Thoreau**

I woke today to the sound of a chainsaw. A neighbour is fell-
ing the row of gum trees on his fence line. There may be
ten or twenty eucalypts in the row. I can hear the chainsaw
grinding and slicing and through the kitchen window see the
bucketed arm of a yellow bulldozer pushing over a tree, and
then another. It snaps and crashes to the ground and the sound

is reverberating across the paddock. I guess he wants the wood but the act seems wanton to me and I mourn for the trees. I turn up the volume on the radio and switch on the woodheater fan to drown out the noise.

Sitting at a desk all day when life is going on outside isn't easy. The seasons are turning, the jobs are too, and I wonder if those things are having an effect on me, like Marilyn and Monroe who sense the day is ending, or the swallows when they leave. Life moves in its own way without a plan. It's Audrey's eightieth summer this year. Leigh is getting married. Annie now shares her farm with Jen. Garagistes, Luke's new restaurant, opened to rave reviews in the national press, while Rodney's Agrarian Kitchen is more successful than he and his wife Severine had ever imagined. At eighty, Les packed up his potter's studio and moved to New South Wales but I can always find his jewels on Lulworth Beach and see his cupped hands holding them. The raspberry plants Libby gave me when they were just sticks are now laden with berries ripe for picking. Richard sold his vineyard and is holidaying this year in Peru. Rose's latest doorstep gift was a bucket of garden macadamia nuts. Lizzie is finally coming to visit from London. Viv still uses her hil-barn hessian bag for carrying her laptop in sunny Gran Canaria where she found her home. Glen has had a baby girl. And Marcelle and I have just found each other on Facebook: 'Hil darling, are you EVER coming to London? If not, why not?'

I want to see her—to tell her that, yes, I have loved again—but it's not a love that is easy to leave. I am connected to the day turning, to the cycle of living, of growing and reaping and, in that union, feel no need to escape. Although I live in the shadow of a church and share its landscape, I have never felt the urge to enter it. My sense of direction is here and (hopefully this makes sense to you) from here it is infinite. In staying in one place I have opened up my world to a flood of probabilities. Life no longer feels starved but abundant. The lemon smile, the fence line, a bend in the road, the arched eyebrow of my mountain and wide veranda view that frames my existence in this stretched valley beneath an ever-changing sky where life ripens and decays . . . this is my eternal, my necessaries in life, and the story of seven summers.

There's an email from Margaret, a loyal hilbarner: 'The girls were overjoyed to recognise the red van driving up the driveway: *Mum! I think it's hilbarn!* We didn't realise how much we've missed you, till then. We've had an abundant summer veggie garden this year, which now is pretty well dormant, so bring on hilbarn!'

I love how hilbarn *is* us—Hil and Barn—yet also exists *outside* of us and that our small business is still growing without being pushed. We do what we do because of where we live and how we want to be together. It's as simple a life recipe as that.

Barn is in his paddock across the road. He looks like the Man from Snowy River except he's riding a mower instead of a horse. He's seen his lady writer in the Nuns' House window, stands up in his seat and tips his hat towards me. We make each other feel warm like sunshine and we are happy living however many summers we may have.

Not that Barn and I do days, birthdays, anniversaries, or even New Year's Day. In how we are, every day seems to have a similar weight. It's how I imagine Jack and Kerouac's days to be, as they amble their slow-motion way up the paddock along the same well-trodden alpaca track to eat the finely sliced apple from my fingertips. There's a sense that there are no Sundays in their world, yet that every day might be a Sunday. Summer and winter, day and night, sun up and moon down.

I'd heard Peter Cundall talking on the radio about the Lalla apple and how he wasn't sure if you could still get them or even if they were still around. They used to be exported to Europe in great quantities before the Common Market came in but you don't see them on sale in any of the orchards or grocers in town, and few of the old Lalla orchards remain. I phoned Alvaro, who thought their friend Chris Olsen might know; he owned quite a bit of land in Lalla. Chris thought if they were anywhere it would be on a couple of old apple trees on top of the hill in an old orchard just opposite the Pear Walk.

'You're welcome to have a look,' he said. 'Feel free to pick some pears while you're there. The trees are at the top of the hill, next to two big old oak trees.'

I stopped the car where Chris had directed, and climbed over the gate into a paddock fenced by an avenue of old pear trees bearing golden teardrops of ripe pears. I started to fill a basket but the sun was dipping behind the softly draped hills and I decided to press on up the slope. The cow paddock opened up into a north-facing field with views of Lalla and beyond. A creek ran through the middle and old huts were calling me in to fossick, but I'd spotted the oak trees ahead on the brow of the hill. As I caught my breath at the top I noticed the trees were gnarled and ancient with views in every direction over a piece of land turning back to nature. There were no apples, the season was over, and the possums had probably done all the picking to be had. I would have to be patient and wait for next year to taste the Lalla apple in Lalla.

*Lalla apple fruit crate label. (Tasmanian Archive and Heritage Office)*

*who you are is*

*where you are*

# READING LIST

## Books I am glad to have met

Wendell Berry, *The Art of the Commonplace: The agrarian essays of Wendell Berry*, Counterpoint, Berkeley, 2002.

*The Countryman* VXXIII No 1 1941 April–May–June, edited and published by J.W. Robertson Scott, Idbury, Oxfordshire.

Peter Cundall, *The Practical Australian Gardener*, Penguin, Camberwell, 1990.

Andy Goldsworthy, *Wall at Storm King*, Thames & Hudson, London, 2000.

*The Organic Gardener's Complete Guide to Vegetables and Fruits*, Rodale Press, 1982.

William Hazlitt, The Spirit of the Age, Grant Richards, London, first published 1825.

Rosemary Hemphill, *Fragrance and Flavour: The growing and use of herbs*, Angus & Robertson, Sydney, 1959.

A.C. Irvine, *Central Cookery Book*, St David's Park Publishing, Hobart, first published 1930.

Susan Irvine, *Rosehips & Crabapples: A rose-lover's diary*, Lantern, 2007.

Meredith Kirton, *Dig*, Murdoch Books, Sydney, 2003.

Stanley Kunitz with Genine Lentine, *The Wild Braid: A poet reflects on a century in the garden*, W.W. Norton & Company, New York, 2005.

Griselda Lewis (ed.), *Handbook of Crafts*, Edward Hulton, 1960.

Stirling Macoboy, *What Flower Is That?*, Lansdowne Press, Sydney, first published 1969.

*The Portfolios of Ansel Adams*, A New York Graphic Society Book, Little Brown and Company, Boston, 1981.

*RHS Good Plant Guide*, Dorling Kindersley, London, 1998.

*The Rubáiyát of Omar Khayyám, The Astronomer-Poet of Persia*, translated by Edward Fitzgerald, Collins, London & Glasgow, first published in 1859.

John Seymour with Will Sutherland, *The New Complete Book of Self-Sufficiency*, Dorling Kindersley, London, 2003.

Nigel Slater, *Appetite*, Fourth Estate, London, 2000.

William Strunk Jr. and E.B. White, *The Elements of Style*, illustrated by Maira Kalman, Penguin, New York, 2000.

*The Tao Box*, Chronicle Books, San Francisco, 2002.

Margaret Tassell, *Rural Launceston Heritage Study: Report of the Queen Victoria Museum and Art Gallery*, QVMAG, Launceston, 2000.

Henry D. Thoreau, *Walden: An annotated edition*, edited by Walter Harding, Houghton Mifflin, Boston & New York, 1995.

*The 21st Birthday Cookery Book of the Country Women's Association in Tasmania*, Penguin, Camberwell, first published 1957.

Edna Walling, *Country Roads: The Australian roadside*, Pioneer Design Studio, Lilydale, Victoria, 1985.

Dave Watts, *Field Guide to Tasmanian Birds*, Reed New Holland, Sydney, 2002.

Sally Wise, *A Year in a Bottle*, ABC Books, Sydney, 2008.